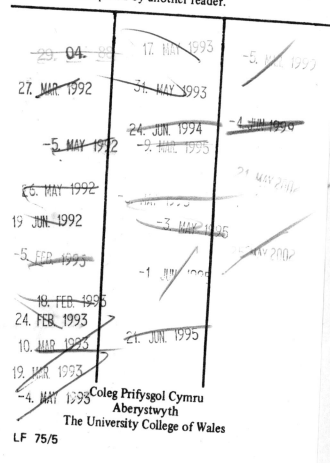

PUBLICATIONS OF THE FACULTY OF ARTS
OF THE UNIVERSITY OF MANCHESTER

No. 21

NATURE AND REASON
IN THE *DECAMERON*

NATURE AND REASON IN THE *DECAMERON*

by

R. HASTINGS

MANCHESTER
UNIVERSITY PRESS

Published by the University of Manchester at

THE UNIVERSITY PRESS

Oxford Road, Manchester M13 9PL

ISBN 0 7190 1281 3

Printed in Great Britain by Butler & Tanner Ltd, Frome and London

CONTENTS

CONTENTS

PREFACE

The main concern of this book is the role of reason in the *Decameron* as a civilising force that guides and controls the satisfaction of natural instinct. The implications and significance of the subject are lost if it is considered in a vacuum, and for that reason I have tried to set it in its proper context. This exercise required a brief outline of existing critical opinion on the historical position of the *Decameron* and on the question of the morality of the work, an indication of the extent of Boccaccio's understanding of human nature and of his objective appraisal of human society in this collection of tales, and a consideration of the major characteristics of the resulting sense of moral values. After this come a definition of the place and function of reason within this framework, and an interpretation of the distinctive notion of virtue that arises from it. These are followed by the examination of a number of particular moral issues, which is designed principally to verify and elucidate the central point by reference to specific example, and by a conclusion that reviews the body of evidence presented in the rest of the book, with the intention of corroborating the earlier suggestion that the *Decameron* occupies an intermediate position between the Middle Ages and the Renaissance. The book also contains an appendix on discussion groups, and an index of all main references. To assist those who do not read Italian or Latin, I have included in the footnotes translations of all the passages taken from Boccaccio's works. The versions used are my own. There is a good modern English version of the *Decameron* by G. H.

McWilliam (published by Penguin Books Ltd, Harmonds-worth, 1972), but there is to my knowledge no adequate complete translation of the Latin works.

I should like to thank Professor T. G. Griffith for the valuable help and advice provided at every stage in the writing and publication of this book. My thanks are also due in large measure to Mrs N. Stålhammer for her patience and efficiency in typing the manuscript.

I

MIDDLE AGES OR RENAISSANCE?

The work of Boccaccio as a whole, and the *Decameron* in particular, have been the subject of much careful critical reappraisal since De Sanctis[1] first hailed him broadly and unreservedly as the impudent, rebellious herald of the Renaissance. As usual, De Sanctis had instinctively sensed the more vital and significant aspects of the author under his consideration, but tended to concentrate on these to the exclusion of all else, thereby producing an unacceptably monolithic and one-sided image of Boccaccio, an oversimplified and consequently somewhat misleading picture. The most obvious omission from De Sanctis's assessment of Boccaccio was a proper examination of his medieval heritage and of its enduring influence on his attitudes as a man, and on his techniques as an artist: a deficiency which Branca[2] amply rectified, and for which indeed he would seem to have overcompensated. Petronio's reply to Branca's book[3] set out to correct the perspective once more, and finally hit the right sort of balance between the two extremes.

It is thus easier now to see the 'medieval' and 'Renaissance' aspects of Boccaccio in their correct proportions, and to envisage him as the transitional figure he really was: a man who was shaped and formed by medieval

[1] F. De Sanctis, *Storia della letteratura italiana*, edited by M. T. Lanza, Feltrinelli, Milan, 1950 (pp. 276 and 339).

[2] V. Branca, *Boccaccio medievale*, Sansoni, Florence, 1956; and 'Giovanni Boccaccio', in *Letteratura Italiana (Orientamenti Culturali): I Maggiori* (1), Marzorati, Milan, 1956.

[3] G. Petronio, 'La posizione del *Decameron*', in *Rassegna della letteratura italiana*, 1957, No. 2, pp. 189–207.

society and education but who lived in an age of fundamental change and development; who not only reflected
but also to a great extent informed and influenced those
changes; and in whom it is ultimately the progressive and
innovatory elements (the so-called 'Renaissance' ones), be
they artistic, social or moral, that appear the more valid,
meaningful and enduring. It is, for instance, his spirit of
worldliness and humanity that is perhaps Boccaccio's
most abiding quality as a man; and it is for such reasons
as this that we tend naturally to remember him still above
all (though not now solely in the way De Sanctis did) as
the forerunner of the Renaissance rather than as the child
of the Middle Ages that he also undoubtedly was.

However, it is at least questionable whether the
application of such generic labels as 'medieval' and
'Renaissance' to transitional figures like Boccaccio and
Petrarch can be considered either useful or appropriate
beyond a certain point; and it seems wiser in the circumstances to relinquish the attempt to pigeonhole Boccaccio, to categorise him as a typical representative of a
particular social and cultural tradition (with the inevitable distortion and misrepresentation that ensue when
the subject is an elusive one that defies pat definitions, as
here), and to concentrate attention instead, initially at
least, on the more salient characteristics of the author
himself.

II

A QUESTION OF MORALS

In the case of the *Decameron* the general discussion of its 'medieval' and 'Renaissance' features has been supplemented by the more specific, but related, question of the 'morality' (or otherwise) of the book: an issue that forms an integral part of the debate already described, but which also contains implications of a somewhat different nature. The old charges of immorality and imputations of moral decadence, indicative of rigid and puritanical attitudes, against which Boccaccio defended himself in the Introduction to Day IV, and in the Conclusion of the *Decameron*, are of course no longer accepted seriously. Another similar criticism of Boccaccio on moral grounds was the charge of frivolity, and again it is one of which he was aware at the time:

Né dubito punto che non sien di quelle ancor che diranno le cose dette esser troppo piene e di motti e di ciance e mal convenirsi ad uno uom pesato e grave aver così fattamente scritto.[4]

The *Decameron* was held to lack seriousness of purpose, and Boccaccio himself to be not so much *im*moral as simply *a*moral, devoid of all moral sense, a writer whose only concern in life was pleasure and amusement. The *Decameron* was just frivolous entertainment, not edifying

[4] 'I have no doubt that there will also be some of you who say that the things I tell of are too full of jests and quips, and that it ill befits a man of weight and gravity to write of such matters.' The passage occurs in the Conclusion of the *Decameron*; see p. 1243 of V. Branca's edition, Le Monnier, Florence, 1965. All subsequent references are to this edition, the text of which is used in all quotations.

or instructive in any way. This image of Boccaccio as a superficial writer, a pure entertainer without a serious thought in his head, survived to a certain extent in De Sanctis, who painted Boccaccio as carefree and unthinking, bent only on amusing and delighting his readers.[5] But this estimate too has been found wanting, and has been subjected to radical revision.

In defence against the charge of immorality it has, moreover, been argued that Boccaccio's attitude is essentially an impartial one that follows no moral line whatsoever, either salutary or corrupting, because he is too objective and detached ever to commit himself. This defence against accusations of immorality often resolved itself into an attempt to explain Boccaccio's attitude in aesthetic terms, by arguing that Boccaccio undoubtedly had moral values but that he did not choose to express them in the *Decameron*, because his preoccupations here were exclusively artistic, his only scruples aesthetic ones. This idea too is found in De Sanctis.[6] But again the consensus of critical opinion has moved away from such a position. It is recognised that Boccaccio is impartial to the extent that he seldom appears to have a particular axe to grind (though an exception should perhaps be made here of his criticisms of the medieval clergy). But it can no longer be maintained that Boccaccio is so completely impartial that he never expresses approval or disapproval, as a multitude of observations and opinions of an explicitly moral nature, expressed either personally by the author himself (in the *Proemio*, the Introductions to Day I and to Day IV, and in the Conclusion of the work), or indirectly through his narrators in the course of the actual telling of the tales, will bear witness. Once this is accepted, it becomes

[5] F. De Sanctis, *Storia della letteratura italiana*, Milan, 1950 (pp. 316–17).
[6] *Ibid.*, p. 280.

impossible to argue convincingly that Boccaccio's only preoccupations are aesthetic. It remains indisputable that artistic scruples have a very high place in his order of priorities, but the view of Boccaccio as a 'pure' artist is no longer a tenable one, any more than it is in the case of Ariosto, to cite a parallel example.

It has therefore become increasingly acknowledged that Boccaccio adopts a clear moral stand in the *Decameron*, and that a very definite sense of moral values emerges from it, albeit of a very different nature from many of the more conventional moral values of the late Middle Ages; that his objectivity and detachment do not eradicate all moral sense, but rather ensure that moral judgements, when they *are* delivered, are not biased or prejudiced but open-minded, just and fair. Sapegno,[7] Petronio,[8] Auerbach,[9] Branca,[10] Scaglione,[11] Givens[12] and others have all in their separate ways contributed to the analysis of the nature, development and presentation of Boccaccio's moral views in the *Decameron*.

This recognition of the moral content of the *Decameron* requires careful qualification, however, for Boccaccio is not pontificating or preaching to his readers; he is not at pains to thrust his message down our throats. He is

[7] N. Sapegno, *Il Trecento (Storia letteraria d'Italia)*, Vallardi, Milan, 1966 (see chapter 6, 'Il Boccaccio'); and *Storia letteraria del Trecento*, Ricciardi, Milan and Naples, 1963.

[8] G. Petronio, *Il Decameron*, Laterza, Bari, 1935; and 'La posizione del *Decameron*', in *Rassegna della letteratura italiana*, 1957, No. 2, pp. 189–207.

[9] E. Auerbach, *Mimesis*, translated by W. Trask, Princeton University Press, 1953 (see chapter 9, 'Frate Alberto').

[10] V. Branca, *Boccaccio medievale*, Florence, 1956; and 'Giovanni Boccaccio', in *Letteratura Italiana (Orientamenti Culturali): I Maggiori* (1), Milan 1956.

[11] A. Scaglione, *Nature and Love in the late Middle Ages*, University of California Press, Berkeley and Los Angeles, 1963.

[12] A. Givens, *La dottrina d'amore nel Boccaccio*, G. D'Anna, Messina and Florence, 1968.

seldom outspoken, either in praise of virtue or in his censure of vice, and although he does express himself openly on a number of occasions, both personally and through his narrators, he chooses more often than not to refrain from explicit comment. Those judgements that *are* expressed are allowed to emerge naturally from the material of the work itself. They are a natural consequence of the author's contemplation of human life and of his reflections upon it. The moral observations of the narrators arise spontaneously from the events of the stories they tell, and are never allowed to predominate; and Boccaccio's own individual pronouncements are very limited, and are mainly in answer to direct criticism. For the rest, he is content to let the message remain implicit. He simply tells the tales, and lets the facts speak for themselves. And the result, of course, is that the moral message of the *Decameron* is more persuasive than it would have been if he had insisted on spelling it out repeatedly to us.

The successful presentation of this message is therefore a consequence of Boccaccio's classical instinct for restraint, discretion and moderation. And the reason it remains largely implicit is that to edify and instruct are never his main aim in the *Decameron*. Although his own sense of values is inevitably reflected in the stories he tells, and in the judgements he gives, and although that sense of values now appears to us to be of profound significance for the history of the development of European civilisation and culture, Boccaccio's primary aim is not moral or didactic. His principal concern *is* entertainment; and, apart from this, his other main preoccupation *is* aesthetic. Moral considerations are usually subordinate to these two, and are never taken *too* seriously. And again the moral stand is more acceptable for being subordinate in this way, in contrast to the tedious and unconvincing moralising of the *Amorosa Visione* and the *Ninfale d'Ameto*.

Once the question of morality can be seen in proper perspective—in its rightful place both in the scheme of Boccaccio's priorities and in the long, hesitant and complex transition from Middle Ages to Renaissance—it becomes possible to focus attention once more on the central issues in the moral order of the *Decameron* without occasioning the sort of misinterpretation that had accompanied the earlier and rather sweeping generalisations of De Sanctis. Here too De Sanctis had already pinpointed the most crucial aspect, which he rightly identified as the role of nature.[13] It remained for later critics to adjust the focus, and to complete the picture by more detailed and specific research. In order to establish the continuity of the *Decameron* with the medieval literary tradition of moral didacticism, Branca[14] has taken a more general view of the moral aspect of the work than most, and indicated the existence of a 'moral architecture' of the stories, a grouping of the tales in such a way that the overall arrangement of the subject-matter and development of the themes from day to day imply a conscious progression from vice to virtue. Obviously this is strongly suggestive of an awareness on Boccaccio's part of the moral import of the book, especially as a similar observation can be made of the *cornice*, the narrative frame within which Boccaccio sets his collection of *novelle*.

The company resolves to escape from the horrors of the plague in Florence, and from the viciousness and degradation of their fellow citizens, in order to preserve their own health and virtue. (Mental sickness and health are

[13] F. De Sanctis, *Storia della letteratura italiana*, Milan, 1950 (pp. 316–17 and 321).

[14] V. Branca, *Boccaccio medievale*, Florence, 1956 (chapter 1, 'Tradizione medievale').

thus a natural reflection of their physical counterparts.)
The narrators therefore leave the corrupt and disease-
ridden city, which has been visited by pestilence, possibly
even as a divine punishment for the sins of its inhabitants,[15]
and where the terrible devastations wrought by the
plague have caused further moral decline, so that all
standards of virtue and decency are overthrown, bar-
barism and savagery are rampant, vice and corruption
rife, and the whole fabric of society is crumbling as the
community dissolves into primitive selfishness and anarchy; and they go instead to the clean air and tranquil
surroundings of the country, where, in the seclusion of
the villas, they build for themselves once more an ordered
and civilised way of life, where a genuine sense of community is regained, where co-operation between indi-
viduals, consideration for others and a feeling of mutual
respect are restored, where decency and decorum are re-
established. This development reaches its climax on the
last day, when all the narrators compete in a spirit of
friendly rivalry to outdo one another in narrating tales of
conspicuous virtue and altruism.

The parallel to the pattern suggested by the architecture
of the stories themselves is clearly recognisable: the over-
coming of vice (the corruption of Florence) and fortune
(the plague) through love and intelligence (men and
women, loved and loving, together in the country, exercising their wits and improving their minds in discussion,
conversation and story-telling, thereby ennobling their

---

[15] See the Introduction to Day I; the plague is: '. . . o per operazione
de' corpi superiori o per le nostre inique opere da giusta ira di Dio a
nostra correzione mandata sopra i mortali, . . .' (*Decameron*, p. 13). '. . .
descended upon mortal men, either through the influence of the heavenly
bodies, or else as a punishment for our sinful deeds, and a mark of God's
wrath, . . .' The idea is repeated shortly afterwards: '. . . l'ira di Dio a
punire le iniquità degli uomini con quella pestilenza . . .' (p. 18). '. . . the
wrath of God, which by this pestilence punishes the iniquities of men . . .'

spirits, developing a sense of moral responsibility and inspiring themselves with virtue: a reflection of the humanist belief in the salutary moral effects of education and culture). The progression discernible in the stories, and that in the *cornice* both culminate in the telling of the stories of the last day, for the exemplary moral nature of these tales not only completes the moral architecture of the stories themselves, it is also a sign of the increased virtue and responsibility of the tellers. The progression from vice to virtue in the architecture of the stories, and that of the *cornice*, are each in their own way a reflection of the general sense of moral purification, a cleansing of the spirit, an expunging from the conscience of all guilt and remorse, which Boccaccio feels within him as a result of the emotional catharsis described in the *Proemio*—his release from the unhappy passion for the legendary Fiammetta.

Critics other than Branca have concentrated their attention on the avenue of investigation indicated by De Sanctis: the role of nature in the moral order of the *Decameron*. Sapegno,[16] Petronio[17] and Auerbach[18] explored Boccaccio's legitimisation of nature and his defence of the free indulgence of natural instincts and desires. Scaglione[19] has since concentrated on the place of Boccaccio's naturalism in the evolution of late medieval thought, envisaging the naturalism of medieval thinking, in which Boccaccio's ideas are rooted, as the necessary preface to the fully developed naturalism of the Renaissance. Givens,[20] in turn, has concerned herself with an examination of the interpretation of love in Boccaccio and his predecessors, both as a chivalrous and literary convention (courtly love) and as a natural force.

[16] See note 7 above.   [17] See note 8 above.   [18] See note 9 above.
[19] See note 11 above.   [20] See note 12 above.

III

UNDERSTANDING MAN

The first significant point to emerge from a closer scrutiny of Boccaccio's moral values is that they are the product of a deep understanding of human nature and human needs, an understanding that derives from the new degree of intellectual objectivity that he attains in the writing of the *Decameron*, and from his consequently detached consideration of human behaviour and human affairs. This objectivity in turn reflects Boccaccio's general maturity of outlook at the time of composition: the serenity and composure, sanity and wisdom, equanimity and inner harmony of spirit that were to become such typical features of the rationalism and classicism of Renaissance art, and that in Boccaccio's case mark the culmination of a process of development through the earlier works, which still retain, especially in the initial stages of his career, a more obviously medieval flavour, and more clearly apprehensible currents of psychological instability and emotional disturbance (characteristics which were to return all too soon after the composition of the *Decameron*).[21]

The measure of mental equilibrium and stability thus achieved allows Boccaccio to view life and humanity from a distance, to get everything into perspective, to see it whole. It enables him to explore the root causes of human behaviour, to discover what it is that makes us act as we do. It brings him to the realisation that we are all conditioned by our heredity and environment, that we are for the most part predictable products of our surroundings

[21] See note 37 below.

and our background, that our character, our attitudes, customs and beliefs are all largely determined by the nature of our own particular *ambiente*: the country, society, class, civilisation and culture to which we belong. It brings him above all to the conviction that man is a natural being, akin to the rest of creation, subject to the same laws of nature that control the animal kingdom as a whole (a world of which he is himself a part), and that constitute the basic realities of all existence; that his actions are influenced by predetermined patterns of instinct and impulse, which nature has bred into him and which it is scarcely possible to suppress or deny.

It becomes apparent to him that human beings are already subject to these laws long before they become accountable to the laws of men, and that nature's law is ever the stronger: whenever social laws and customs are artificial and unnatural, whenever they seek to repress natural instincts, basic needs and desires, they are bound to be broken. Nature will out; she cannot be denied; she always finds an outlet in the end. Attempts to go against nature, to impose unnatural standards of conduct on men and women, in the name of a 'higher' social code or moral law that fails to take nature into account, and that consequently contradicts or runs counter to the natural laws on which it is superimposed, are inevitably doomed to failure, because they are trying to make us go against our own selves, to deny our very natures. And not only are they impossible, they also cause needless frustration and suffering (for instance, the distress caused to women in love by confining them to their chambers, and depriving them of the satisfaction of their desires, at which Boccaccio protests in the *Proemio*).[22] And furthermore they result in hypocrisy and dissimulation, in vain attempts to cover up

[22] See the passage from the *Proemio* quoted on pp. 56-7.

and to conceal our failure to adhere to the impossible standards of conduct we have set ourselves. (The medieval clergy are, in Boccaccio's eyes, the worst culprits here.)

These are facts that not only emerge from the material of the stories but are, in addition, made plain to us by the author himself on several occasions in clear and unequivocal statements:

La qual dicendo, ad un'ora vi mosterrò chente sia la sciocchezza di questi cotali, e quanto ancora sia maggiore quella di coloro li quali, sé più che la natura possenti estimando, si credono quello con dimostrazioni favolose potere che essi non possono, e sforzansi d'altrui recare a quello che essi sono, non patendolo la natura di chi è tirato.[23]

... alle cui leggi, cioè della natura, voler contastare, troppe gran forze bisognano, e spesse volte non solamente invano ma con grandissimo danno del faticante s'adoperano.[24]

Boccaccio perceives that the social codes and moral laws of medieval society are governed by three main principles: religious asceticism (the values of medieval Christianity), honour and respectability (the code of honour of the old feudal aristocracy, and the concern for respectability of the middle classes), and money and profit (the often exclusive preoccupation of the *popolo grasso* with practical and financial matters, with the accumulation of wealth and possessions, whereby money becomes the foundation of all values, the touchstone by which the merits of all things are assessed). Each of these is in its way artificial, each fails to take human instincts and

[23] Day II, story 10 (*Decameron*, p. 295). The speaker is Dioneo. 'In my story I shall show you how foolish such folk are, and also how much more foolish are those who think themselves more powerful than nature, who with abstruse arguments convince themselves that they can perform the impossible, and who try to force others to be like them, even though the nature of the subject will not allow it.'

[24] Introduction to Day IV (*Decameron*, p. 459). The speaker is Boccaccio himself. See the translation of the passage on pp. 29–30 (note 44).

emotions sufficiently into account and each is thus infringed and contravened by the natural forces it seeks to repress. The tale of Masetto and the nuns (the first story of Day III) reveals the shortcomings of the ascetic ideal of the Church:

Bellissime donne, assai sono di quegli uomini e di quelle femine che sì sono stolti, che credono troppo bene che, come ad una giovane è sopra il capo posta la benda bianca e in dosso messale la nera cocolla, che ella più non sia femina né più senta de' feminili appetiti se non come se di pietra l'avesse fatta divenire il farla monaca: e se forse alcuna cosa contra questa lor credenza n'odono, così si turbano come se contra natura un grandissimo e scelerato male fosse stato commesso, non pensando né volendo aver rispetto a se medesimi, li quali la piena licenzia di poter far quel che vogliono non può saziare, né ancora alle gran forze dell'ozio e della solitudine. E similmente sono ancora di quegli assai che credono troppo bene che la zappa e la vanga e le grosse vivande e i disagi tolgano del tutto a' lavoratori della terra i concupiscibili appetiti e rendan loro d'intelletto e d'avvedimento grossissimi. Ma quanto tutti coloro che così credono sieno ingannati, mi piace, poi che la reina comandato me l'ha, non uscendo della proposta fatta da lei, di farvene più chiare con una piccola novelletta.[25]

[25] *Decameron*, pp. 318–19. 'Fairest ladies, there are a good many men and women who are so stupid that they believe implicitly that when a young woman puts on a white veil and a black habit she is no longer a woman, and does not feel womanly desires, as if she had been turned to stone by being made a nun; and if anyone happens to challenge this belief they become as distressed as if some great and wicked crime had been perpetrated against nature, not thinking, and not wishing to admit, that their own desires are never quenched, even though they are free to do as they wish; and failing to consider the powerful effects of idleness and solitude. And similarly there are a great many who are convinced that breaking clods, digging earth, eating coarse food and leading a hard life take away all the peasant's lustful desires and make him dull and slow-witted. But as the queen has commanded me to speak, I should like to tell you a little story that, without wandering from the theme she has proposed, will show you just how wrong these people are in their beliefs.'

And the message is reinforced by the story of Balducci, in the Introduction to Day IV, where the father is forced ruefully to concede his inability to override the natural instincts of his son: '. . . e sentì incontanente più aver di forza la natura che il suo ingegno; e pentessi d'averlo menato a Firenze'.[26] The tales of Tancredi, Ghismonda and Guiscardo (the first story of Day IV), and of Lizio da Valbona and his daughter Caterina (the fourth story of Day V), expose the inadequacy of prevalent social notions of what constitutes honour and respectability. And the inhuman nature of an order of values founded on money alone is uncovered by the triumphant marriage of the wealthy widow Monna Giovanna to the impoverished Federigo, despite her family's objections (the ninth story of Day V):

La quale, poi che piena di lagrime e d'amaritudine fu stata alquanto, essendo rimasa ricchissima e ancora giovane, più volte fu da' fratelli costretta a rimaritarsi; la quale, come che voluto non avesse, pur veggendosi infestare, ricordatasi del valore di Federigo e della sua magnificenzia ultima, cioè d'avere ucciso un così fatto falcone per onorarla, disse a' fratelli: 'Io volentieri, quando vi piacesse, senza rimaritarmi mi starei; ma se a voi pur piace che io marito prenda, per certo io non ne prenderò mai alcuno altro, se io non ho Federigo degli Alberighi.'

Alla quale i fratelli, faccendosi beffe di lei, dissero: 'Sciocca, che è ciò che tu di'? come vuoi tu lui che non ha cosa del mondo?'

A' quali ella rispose: 'Fratelli miei, io so bene che così è come voi dite, ma io voglio avanti uomo che abbia bisogno di ricchezza, che ricchezza che abbia bisogno d'uomo.'

Li fratelli, udendo l'animo di lei e conoscendo Federigo da

---

[26] *Decameron*, p. 455. '. . . and he saw at once that his wits were of no avail against nature, and he regretted bringing him to Florence.'

molto, quantunque povero fosse, sì come ella volle, lei con tutte le sue ricchezze gli donarono.[27]

The inescapable conclusion to be drawn from such examples, Boccaccio implies, is that man is not always a purely rational creature, a completely free agent with a mind and a will entirely his own, fully able to order and determine his behaviour as he sees fit, completely responsible for his actions, and with absolute freedom of choice between right and wrong. He has not in fact complete control over his behaviour, because he is also a creature of instinct and impulse who often simply cannot *help* acting as he does, because his reactions and responses are conditioned by the forces of his natural environment in a simple chain of cause and effect that makes him act in a way that is often to a large extent automatic and foreseeable.

These are ideas to which Boccaccio returns in the *Genealogie Deorum Gentilium Libri* and in the *Buccolicum Carmen*. The relevant passages from the *Genealogie Deorum Gentilium Libri* are:

Nam, ut cytharista variis ex fidibus, aliis lentius, aliis vero protensius tractis, his gravem, acutum illis tinnitum reddentibus, docta manu plectroque ex tam discordantibus tonis reddit suavissimam armoniam, sic et natura parens, cui inexhauste

---

[27] *Decameron*, pp. 677–8. 'After she had wept bitterly for some little while, her brothers repeatedly urged her to remarry, since she had been left very rich and was still young; and though she would have preferred not to, as they were so insistent she recalled to mind the worthy Federigo and his recent act of generosity in killing such a fine falcon to do her honour, and so she said to her brothers, "With your consent, I would prefer not to marry again, but if you still want me to take a husband let me make it clear that I shall never accept anyone other than Federigo degli Alberighi."

'Her brothers answered mockingly, "What nonsense is this? How can you possibly want a man without a penny to his name?"

'To which she replied, "My brothers, I am well aware that what you say is true, but I would rather have a good man without wealth than wealth without virtue."

'Seeing that her mind was made up, the brothers, who had known Federigo a long time, poor though he was, gave her to him with all her riches, just as she desired.'

vires et perfectum ingenium est, producit hec peritura diversis officiis apta, ut ex hac officiorum inconvenientia resultet humani generis, circa quod plurimum intenta est, conservatio.

Ergo hinc fit, ut discreto nature ordine hic ex mortalibus nascatur faber lignarius, ille nauta, mercator alius, et quidam sacerdotio apti aut regimini, et non nulli legum latores, presides, poete, phylosophi, seu sublimes theologi. Ex quorum studiis variis tam ingentis multitudinis hominum conservatio resultet necesse est!

Uti incommodum[28] [*sic*] humani corporis inter se differentia qualitate et officio membra a natura rerum apposita sunt, ut ex hac diversitate consistat, uti melodia ex diversitate tonorum, sic et, ut humanum genus perseveret, necesse fuit ad studia inter se differentia gigneremur. Et si ab ipsa natura, que sic celos, sic astrorum orbes et cursus varia etiam agitatione disposuit, agente Deo, ut nullo labore suo ad officia productos varia nos videmus, quis, queso, feliciter audebit ab eo, ad quod natus est, in aliud transitum attentare? Non quidem adeo ignarus sum, quin noverim liberi arbitrii, quo omnes valemus, potentia possimus nature superare vires; quod egisse non nullos legimus. Opus profecto inter raro contingentia numerandum, tam grandi et fere invincibili necessitate trahimur, in quod nascimur! Et si ad diversa gignimur, nascimur alimurque si ea plene peragamus in que trahimur, equidem satis est, nedum in aliud transitum fecisse velimus; quod dum iam dudum frustra temptarent aliqui, id perdidere, quod erant, nec id potuerunt effici, quod querebant.[29]

Boccaccio here envisages nature moulding the capabilities of the individual, endowing different men with different

---

[28] The reading *incommodum* makes no sense: a more plausible interpretation would be *in commodum*.

[29] *Genealogie Deorum Gentilium Libri*, edited by V. Romano, Laterza, Bari, 1951: book xv, chapter 10 (vol. ii, pp. 775–6).
'For, as the lutanist, by skilful use of hand and plectrum, composes the sweetest harmony from the discordant tones of the various strings, some being more tightly stretched than others, to give a range of deep

aptitudes, so that each can fulfil the particular role in society to which he is by nature called: a pattern which, he considers, is calculated to ensure the preservation of the human race. He concludes, therefore, that we should devote ourselves to the cultivation of those talents given us by nature, and follow our natural calling, rather than try to become something which we are not. He is thinking principally of his own resolve to become a poet, which he felt nature had intended him to be, rather than a merchant or a lawyer, which his father tried to make him become against his own inclinations. A similar observation occurs in the *Buccolicum Carmen*:

Nascimur in varios actus, quos optima virtus
si sequitur, facili ducetur ad ultima cursu.[30]

---

and high notes, so too mother nature, whose powers are inexhaustible and whose being is perfection, produces different aptitudes in mortal men, that the preservation of mankind, her prime concern, may ensue from the variety of our pursuits.'

'Thus through her wisdom this man is born a carpenter, that a sailor, another a merchant, some are suited to be priests or kings, some lawyers, judges, poets, philosophers or eminent theologians. And the preservation of this vast multitude of men results of necessity from the variety of their occupations.'

'Just as the various parts of the human body are assigned to particular functions by nature for the well-being of the whole, that cohesion may be created from diversity, as in a melody composed of different notes, so too was it essential for the survival of mankind that we be born for different occupations. And if we find that God has directed nature herself, who ordered the very heavens, and the orbits and courses of the stars in their various motions, to form us likewise for different activities, without His direct involvement, who, pray, will venture successfully to became something other than that for which he was born? I am not, indeed, so ignorant that I do not realise that we all have it in us to overcome the forces of nature by the strength of our own free will: we may read of a number of cases where this has happened. [But] it is indeed a rare achievement, so great and well nigh invincible is the constraint that impels us towards that for which we are born! And since we are born, bred and nourished for different pursuits, if we each fully accomplish our own calling, without aspiring to change our sphere of activity, that in itself is quite enough. Some have tried at length and in vain to change themselves, and failed to fulfil their true selves, without becoming what they sought to be.'

[30] *Buccolicum Carmen*, twelfth eclogue, 'Saphos', verses 190–1 (*Opere*

Such insight is very advanced, and far-reaching in its implications. It not only anticipates later Renaissance writers (Montaigne, for example); it already foreshadows Darwin (the theory of evolution, natural selection and the survival of the species), and even the current sciences of behaviourism and ecology. Not, of course, that Boccaccio ever uses anything approaching the technical jargon of more recent times, or even gives concrete expression to concepts like heredity and environment as such. He was writing before the birth of modern science as we know it today, and he was writing as a *novelliere*, not as a scholar. His understanding of human nature and his sense of social perspective are not consciously rationalised, or developed intellectually to any special degree. He advances no system or corporate theory. His is an intuitive understanding, an instinctive awareness, not a rational acquisition; but it is none the less significant for that.

Latine Minori, edited by A. Massèra, Laterza, Bari, 1928, p. 61). 'We are born into various roles, and if we follow them with the utmost determination, we will readily attain our goal.'

IV

THE RELATIVE STANDPOINT

It is this objective understanding of human nature which makes possible that sense of relativism that finds such apt expression in the tale of Melchisedech and the three rings:[31] the ability to see different societies and cultures (and the attitudes and customs which appertain to them) in overall perspective, in their proper relationship one to another, to assess and evaluate each objectively and impartially by viewing from without instead of from the exclusive standpoint of someone so conditioned in attitude and outlook, so committed to the values of his own social environment (in this case to traditional Christian values and beliefs) that he is unable to understand or appreciate those of any other. Boccaccio is thus enabled in the *Decameron* to outgrow his narrowness, to put off for a time the subjectivity and involvement that attended him in his youth, and the prejudices and resentments that beset him in his old age. If attitudes, opinions and beliefs are subjective and inherited, he suggests in the shrewd reply of the Jewish merchant to Saladin,[32] then who am I

[31] Day I, story 3. This was a popular medieval story that existed as a traditional tale in its own right long before Boccaccio incorporated it in the *Decameron*, and the spirit of relativism it contains is not due entirely to Boccaccio's own contribution. But the message of the tale is largely wasted in earlier versions. The *Novellino*, for instance (story 73 in the Gualteruzzi edition, and story 111 in Biagi), gives only a bald schematic outline, and fails to exploit the significance of the Jew's reply. It required a man like Boccaccio, genuinely sympathetic to the spirit of objectivity and tolerance which the *novella* embodies, to make it yield its true potential.

[32] 'E così vi dico, signor mio, delle tre Leggi alli tre popoli date da Dio Padre, delle quali la quistion proponeste: ciascuno la sua eredità, la sua vera Legge e i suoi comandamenti dirittamente si crede avere e

to claim that I am right and you are wrong, that I am good and you are bad? We are simply *different*; and the interesting thing is not to try and establish absolute standards of truth and virtue but to try and see how and why we have come to behave and think as we do, to investigate the nature of the forces that have formed our character and shaped our attitudes. It is noteworthy that the story of Melchisedech is also in its way a convincing study of national character: the disarming way he neutralises Saladin's unvoiced threat by his deliberately evasive reply is typical of the shrewd and wily Jewish moneylenders of medieval Italy. He is a recognisable type, the authentic product of a given social milieu. He is indeed reminiscent of the character in the old Jewish joke who was asked why Jews always answer a question with a question and replied, 'Why shouldn't we?' The similarity of the response is not merely casual: it indicates a reluctance to commit oneself that stems from the caution and circumspection of a victimised minority.

---

fare; ma chi se l'abbia, come degli anelli, ancora ne pende la quistione.' (*Decameron*, p. 78.) '"And so, my lord, concerning the three laws given to the three peoples by God our Father, which were the subject of your question, my answer is that each people believes that its own law is the true law, and that the commandments by which it lives are held by direct inheritance; but, as with the rings, no one has yet discovered who is right."'

V

TOLERANCE

However, for our purpose the most important consequences of Boccaccio's understanding of human nature are the moral implications. Boccaccio's general attitude to the question of morality is, as we would expect in the circumstances, a liberal and broadminded one. His standards are not narrow, rigid, strict, austere: they are tolerant and enlightened. His disposition is kindly and benevolent, compassionate and forbearing, charitable and humane.[33] These reserves of tolerance flow both from the awareness that no man is totally responsible for his acts, because of the way his character is conditioned, and from his sense of relativism, which prompts him, as in the story of Melchisedech, to the proposition that if no one knows who really has the right answer, then we must not condemn others whose rule of life is different from ours. He displays particular tolerance of human weakness and error, through his appreciation of the power of natural instinct, to which all men are subject, and a reluctance to condemn in others the faults and weaknesses which he recognises to be common to all men, including himself: it may be wrong, but none of us is perfect, so who are we to judge? It is an attitude that embodies the substance of three time-honoured maxims: that to understand all is to forgive all; that there, but for the grace of God, go I; and

[33] This is not by any means always true of Boccaccio in his other works, however; it is a feature of the psychological equilibrium of the mature Boccaccio that emerges fully only in the *Decameron* itself, and which seems to have been already disrupted by the time he wrote the *Corbaccio*, where personal prejudices and resentments return with a greater force even than in his early works (see note 37 below, and pp. 59–60).

that to err is human, to forgive divine. And it finds characteristic utterance in Pietro di Vinciolo's forgiveness of his wife's infidelity, because he knows that he himself is not free from blame: '. . . Pietro corre là, vedelo, cognosce lo 'nganno della moglie, con la quale ultimamente rimane in concordia per la sua tristezza.'[34] Pietro's motives are far from being pure and disinterested. His principal concern is to gratify his own homosexual desires with the young man in question. But his words to his wife, upon the discovery of her adultery, indicate that tolerance and understanding also play a part in his forgiveness of her misdemeanours: it is not for her infidelity that he scolds her but rather for her sanctimonious criticisms of other women's adultery when she is herself guilty of the same fault:

. . . alla quale Pietro postosi a seder dirimpetto disse: 'Or tu maladicevi così testé la moglie d'Ercolano e dicevi che arder si vorrebbe e che ella era vergogna di tutte voi: come non dicevi di te medesima? o se di te dir non volevi, come ti sofferiva l'animo di dir di lei, sentendoti quel medesimo aver fatto che ella fatto avea?'[35]

The note of compassion is sounded also in Dioneo's preamble to the tale, where he urges his listeners to temper their mirth with pity for the wife's lover: '. . . liete riderete degli amorosi inganni della sua donna, compassione avendo all'altrui sciagure, dove bisogna'.[36]

There is little in the *Decameron* that could be called

[34] *Decameron*, Day V, story 10, p. 679. '. . . Pietro rushes up, sees him, realises his wife's deception, but in the end agrees to forgive her because of his own iniquity.'

[35] *Decameron*, p. 689. '. . . Pietro sat down in front of her and said, "Now you've just been cursing Ercolano's wife, and saying she deserved to be burnt alive, and that she was a disgrace to her sex. Why didn't you mention yourself? Or, if you didn't want to involve yourself, how could you bring yourself to talk of her when you knew you had done the same thing she had?"'

[36] *Decameron*, p. 680. See the translation of the passage on p. 50 (note 81).

severe censure or violent condemnation. The note of asperity is reserved only for those instances of transgression and wrongdoing that are the fruit of malice, those infringements of the rights of others that are consciously willed, that arise from calculated fraud, from deliberate, malevolent deceit (and again the accusing finger points towards the clergy). It is this quality of tolerance that has so often been mistaken for lack of moral principle, or even for incitement to vice. It is in fact neither of these things. Boccaccio's indulgence of human weakness is compounded of sympathy and understanding, based on the realisation of our common humanity.

VI

THE SECULAR OUTLOOK

The second salient characteristic of Boccaccio's values is that they reflect his essentially secular outlook. His interests and inclinations in the *Decameron* are all wordly ones, and not until later life did he revert to a more conventional ascetic and religious standpoint.[37] It is not that he is irreligious or agnostic here; in matters of belief he was always orthodox. But he is completely unconcerned with the transcendental and metaphysical preoccupations of medieval theology, and he is convinced of the inadequacy of the ascetic moral ideal. His attention is focused on this life, not the next. He is, on the one hand, realistic, mundane, sensible, down-to-earth, with both feet firmly

[37] When the transformation *did* come, however, it was swift and startlingly decisive. Almost the whole of the liberal philosophy of the *Decameron* was revoked, and the book itself was subsequently disowned. Boccaccio's increasing asceticism resulted in a profound revision of his views on nature, love, religion and a number of similar issues. He also manifested signs of personal instability and emotional disturbance (see p. 10), and a growing intolerance (see note 33 above), that contrast strongly with the serenity of spirit, the sympathy and understanding of the author of the *Decameron* itself. These changes began almost as soon as the *Decameron* was finished: the mentality of the author of the *Corbaccio* (written immediately after the *Decameron*) is already very different from the Boccaccio we see reflected in the earlier work.

The whole question of Boccaccio's regression in later life to more prejudiced and ascetic attitudes, and of his increasing insecurity and disturbance, is a vexed one. A number of factors may have contributed: possible personal and emotional trauma (reflected in the bitter invective of the *Corbaccio:* see pp. 59–60); the influence of Petrarch, who was instrumental in converting Boccaccio to a more ascetic outlook, and from whom he absorbed many of the prejudices of the early humanists, as well as the more positive side of the new scholarship (see pp. 59–60 and 77); poverty, loneliness and ill health also took their toll, as did the fear of death and damnation that preyed upon his mind towards the end (though this was not until much later), and which even Petrarch's comfort and encouragement never fully allayed.

planted on the ground; on the other, sensual and pleasure-loving. He has a great curiosity in the world about him, and, above all, an absorbing interest in his fellow man and in the infinite variety yet fundamental similarity of human nature. His universe at this stage is man-centred, not God-centred, a standpoint which is revealed in Filomena's opening remarks in the third story of Day I:

Per ciò che già e di Dio e della verità della nostra Fede è assai bene stato detto, il discendere oggimai agli avvenimenti e agli atti degli uomini non si dovrà disdire, . . .[38]

The remarks should not be taken out of context—their principal function is to introduce the secular story of Melchisedech after two others ostensibly concerning religion—but it is nevertheless expressive of the author's general outlook. The treatment both of the tale of Melchisedech and of the opening story of Ser Ciappelletto is itself a telling illustration of the direction his interests are taking. In both, the focus of attention is transferred from the moral didactic element inherited from the *exemplum* tradition, with its conventional overtones of religious piety, to the more immediate human aspect: the admiration of human intelligence for its own sake.[39] With Ser Ciappelletto, Boccaccio's enthusiasm persists even though the ingenuity displayed involves disrespect for religion: the impiety is criticised but the ingenuity is none the less admired, and the criticism is hence largely token and conventional.[40]

The *Decameron* glows with a love of life and people, a

[38] *Decameron*, p. 74. 'Since our tales have already done justice both to God and to the truth of our faith, it will not be inappropriate if we now come down to the affairs and deeds of men, . . .'

[39] For further consideration of this element in the two stories see chapter XIII, pp. 75–7 (and notes 125 and 127 below), and chapter XVI, p. 94 (and note 155 below).

[40] See p. 66.

keen sense of the joy of living, an appreciation of the good things in life: youth, beauty, health, friendship and love. Because he is a realist Boccaccio does not try to shut out the dark side of life: violence, cruelty, disease and death, pain, distress, poverty and old age. All these things were in many ways more inescapably real and immediate in the Middle Ages than they are today, and Boccaccio accepts them as such, as can be seen both from the pathetic and tragic tales and from the Introduction to Day I, with its grim description of the plague. But his acceptance of the unpleasant side only makes him more appreciative of the attractive side of life, because it makes it seem more precious. And the same applies to his attitude to his fellow men: they are seen in their entirety, warts and all; and they are much more appealing with their defects and shortcomings than they could have been if they were perfect. Such are Boccaccio's allegiances, and underlying them all is the steadfast assertion of the right of every human being to find happiness here and now, while still alive on this earth.

This rejection of the ascetic values of medieval religion for wordly ones is the outstanding early manifestation of that stand of Christian humanism which constitutes one of the principal achievements of Renaissance ethics: the legitimisation of earthly allegiances, human pleasures and secular pursuits, the recognition of the validity of natural human needs, embracing them within the substance of religious faith instead of seeking to deny them, as medieval Christianity, with its uncompromising asceticism, was bound to do. So, for this brief period in his life at least, Boccaccio succeeded in effecting that cherished identification and fusion of human and religious goals that Petrarch strove so long and so vainly to achieve, and which it was only given to the later humanists to consolidate as an enduring acquisition. There is, in the *Decameron*, no longer any sense of shame or guilt or remorse attached to the satisfaction of natural instincts and worldly desires, as there so often is in much medieval literature. There is only a joyful acceptance of them as man's rightful heritage, as something God-given, as something meant to be used and enjoyed to the full.

One of the most persuasive illustrations of this outlook occurs in the *novella* of Rinieri and Elena. Although it is to end on a bitter note, the story opens with an unequivocal assertion of the legitimacy of love as something divinely bestowed and divinely sanctioned:

... e seco estimò colui potersi beato chiamare, al quale Iddio grazia facesse lei potere ignuda nelle braccia tenere.[41]

And the narrators themselves furnish further instances of the same attitude. In the Introduction to Day I, Pampinea proposes that the young ladies invite three young men to accompany them on their country retreat. Neifile says this will cause scandal, but Filomena replies:

'Questo non monta niente; là dov'io onestamente viva né mi rimorda d'alcuna cosa la coscienza, parli chi vuole in contrario: Iddio e la verità l'arme per me prenderanno.'[42]

God will know they have done nothing wrong, and their consciences will be clear. And at the end of the rural sojourn Panfilo insists once more that the company has done nothing wrong in coming to the country, in enjoying the pleasures of fine buildings and gardens,

---

[41] Day VIII, story 7 (*Decameron*, p. 932). '... and he considered that the man to whom God granted favour to hold her naked in his arms could call himself blessed indeed.'

[42] *Decameron*, p. 37. '"That does not matter; if I live a decent life, and my conscience is free from remorse, they can say what they like against me: God and the truth will be on my side."'

exquisite food and wines, and the company of the opposite sex, and in entertaining themselves by the telling of interesting and amusing stories.[43]

[43] In the Conclusion to Day X (*Decameron*, pp. 1234–5): see p. 82.

VII

TO FOLLOW NATURE

Boccaccio's liberal disposition, his tolerance and his rejection of asceticism are all, in their different ways, the result of his own conception of the true quality of human existence. But perhaps the most obvious consequence of all is the persuasion that the one sure and appropriate way to attain the happiness to which all men are entitled is to follow nature. The categoric exhortation to follow nature lies at the very heart of the moral message of the *Decameron*, and justifies the definition of that message as one of 'natural morality'. Whenever a hiatus occurs between social convention and natural human needs Boccaccio advocates a rejection of artificial criteria and an adherence to the natural pattern of life: nature's way is best, and it is right and proper to obey her promptings, and follow her call. It is both foolish and cruel to seek to deny our natural instincts. We should rather give way to them, indulge and satisfy them properly, as Boccaccio himself tells us in the Introduction to Day IV when he addresses his female readers with the words:

E se mai con tutta la mia forza a dovervi in cosa alcuna compiacere mi disposi, ora più che mai mi vi disporrò, per ciò che io conosco che altra cosa dir non potrà alcun con ragione, se non che gli altri e io, che vi amiamo, naturalmente operiamo; alle cui leggi, cioè della natura, voler contastare, troppe gran forze bisognano, e spesse volte non solamente invano ma con grandissimo danno del faticante s'adoperano. Le quali forze io confesso che io non l'ho né d'averle disidero in questo; e se io l'avessi, più tosto ad altrui le presterrei che io per me l'adoperassi.[44]

And this position is supported by the words of Dioneo in the tenth story of Day II.[45] These are the basic facts of life, which we cannot change. We should accept them as part of the existing order of things. We should seek not to resist them but rather to accommodate ourselves to them, to adapt to the circumstances in which we find ourselves. The logical implication of such a view is that instead of trying to adhere to artificial and unworkable moral standards we should attempt to formulate codes of ethics that are based on a proper recognition of human needs, and which seek to secure happiness by the proper satisfaction of natural instincts.

To follow nature was thus a precept that constituted something of a rule of life for Boccaccio, a rule whose principal application was an ethical one but which was not always restricted to a moral context by any means. His distrust of medieval doctors and his preference for natural remedies in the treatment of illness, as revealed in his letters, are another instance of the practical application of the same fundamental principle in matters of health and medicine. In the letter to Mainardo Cavalcanti, written in 1373 about his own poor state of health, he observes:

Remedia nulla michi sunt, nec hic medicus nec medela, etsi sit nulla michi fides in illis: vivo natura et appetitu ducibus.

[44] *Decameron*, p. 459. 'And if ever I resolved to devote myself to pleasing you in anything, now I shall do so more than ever, because I know that we who love you are following nature, and that no one can reasonably say otherwise; for to try and oppose these laws—the laws of nature, that is—demands exceptional powers, and even then the effort is often in vain and the effects extremely harmful. And I confess that I neither have such powers, nor do I wish to have them; and if I did possess them, I would rather give them away than use them myself.'

[45] See chapter III, p. 12, and note 23 above.

And later on in the same letter he tells us that he was unwilling to call a doctor during a recent attack for this very reason:

Hortantur ut medicum advocem, quod ego tanquam superfluum aspernabar, consuetus nature accidentium quorumcunque in diem usque illam curam permittere.[46]

The study of medicine in the Middle Ages had been one of the principal victims of the abuse of scholasticism. Its practitioners had lost touch with the realities of their profession, and were better versed in philosophy, dialectic and rhetoric than in the diagnosis and treatment of the physical afflictions of the human body. Hence most doctors were mere pedants who clothed their ignorance in learned but meaningless technical Latin jargon, and many indeed were unscrupulous charlatans who exploited the gullibility of their patients by extracting exorbitant sums of money from them under false pretences. The attentions of such 'physicians' often did more harm than good (the standard treatments for most ailments were purging and bloodletting), and it is not surprising that informed scholars like Boccaccio and Petrarch spoke out against them for meddling in matters they did not understand, and preferred in practice to dispense with their tender ministrations and allow nature to effect her own cure.

---

[46] These passages are taken from *Opere in versi, Corbaccio, In laude di Dante, Prose latine, Epistole,* edited by P. Ricci, Ricciardi, Milan and Naples, 1965, pp. 1234 and 1236.

'I have here no remedies, nor doctor, nor medicine, but I have no faith in them anyway: I live under the guidance of nature and instinct.'

'They [my friends] urged me to call a doctor, which I scorned as useless, for until that day I had been accustomed to allow nature to cure me of any illness.'

VIII

THE ROLE OF REASON

That the advocacy of a willing adherence to nature is a central theme of the moral message of the *Decameron* is, as I have indicated, a fact that has been recognised by a number of critics. But what many have perhaps been reluctant to acknowledge so far is that the satisfaction of natural instinct is only half the message of natural morality in the *Decameron*. An important aspect of the new values that has hitherto received rather less attention than it deserves is the role of reason as a civilising force, as a guide, restrainer and humaniser of basic natural instincts, such as love. Much has been made of Boccaccio's cult of intelligence, but the emphasis is usually laid on the enlistment of intelligence in the *service* of love, and the satisfaction of the lover's desires, not on its possible application as a guide of love and as a curb of natural instinct.

Sapegno is perhaps more aware of this aspect than most, for in his discussion of Boccaccio's cult of intelligence he does advance the view that intelligence is the foundation of virtue in the *Decameron*.[47] But the assertion is never elaborated, or indeed substantiated, and the relationship remains an assumed one only. Petronio suggests that reason may control nature, but he does not envisage this as a moral corrective, merely as a matter of expediency, as a means of attaining one's desired end, whether virtuous or otherwise.[48] Scaglione, moreover,

[47] N. Sapegno, *Il Trecento* (*Storia letteraria d'Italia*), Milan, 1966, chapter 6, pp. 333-9 (and especially p. 333: '... l'esaltazione commossa del nobile intelletto, nel quale è infine il solo fondamento sicuro e la più piena consapevolezza dell' ideale etico').

[48] G. Petronio, *Il Decameron*, Bari, 1935, pp. 43-53 (and especially

actually rejects the idea of reason as a moral restraint, and expresses reservations even concerning Petronio's position.[49] Scaglione recognises that Boccaccio is an important figure in the formulation of a moral order based on nature and reason, which develops gradually as the Renaissance emerges from the Middle Ages, in that he represents to us an order in which nature rules human life, and acknowledges none of the controls which medieval society seeks to impose on it. But, though he distinguishes the interplay of nature and reason as one of the key features of the *Decameron*, he maintains that the emphasis upon reason as a *curb* of nature (as opposed to the exaltation of intelligence as a subordinate and ally of nature, as an aid to the satisfaction of natural instinct) is not yet apparent in Boccaccio himself.[50]

Scaglione's examination of the relationship of the *Decameron* to other expressions of naturalism in the Middle Ages leads him to conclude that, while Boccaccio's ideas are not without precedent in medieval thinking, the expression of his natural morality nevertheless assumes, in the *Decameron*, the form of a single-minded polemic against existing standards; and the result of this polemic is seen to be the excessive stress which Boccaccio places,

p. 45, where Petronio defines Boccaccio's conception of intelligence as 'questa capacità di sottomettere desideri e passioni, morali o immorali, legali o illegali che siano, al dominio della ragione, estrinsecandoli con la più cosciente consapevolezza, senza titubanze, senza scrupoli sciocchi e senza falsi pudori, in una capacità di fermamente e saldamente volere').

[49] A. Scaglione, *Nature and Love in the late Middle Ages*, Berkeley and Los Angeles, 1963, pp. 96–7: 'Yet, the danger of Petronio's interpretation, as I see it, is in the extent to which one is ready to posit the control by reason over the senses and the heart.'

[50] *Ibid.*, p. 96: 'It is . . . the world of "sentiment" serenely fused with reason and the will. Love is, indeed, irrational, but reason follows and serves it, without being quite subjugated by it. . . . But it is not the mature Renaissance, in which love will work more for the ends of reason, its rightful guide, than vice versa.'

in his estimation, upon the free indulgence of natural instinct, and the failure, at this early stage in the evolution of Renaissance naturalism, to envisage the need for rational restraint of some kind, a deficiency which he considers later writers were able to repair. In other words, Boccaccio, being the first to make the break, is forced to go to the other extreme in order to establish his opposition to what had gone before, and so concentrates almost exclusively on the need to follow nature freely, irrespective of all other considerations, especially in matters of love.[51] And the result, in Scaglione's view, is potential anarchy,[52] a prospect which can be averted only by a partial retraction of the call for freedom and a belated compromise with the existing fabric of social convention (and therefore with the very moral order whose inadequacies the *Decameron* exposes, and whose injunctions it openly flouts): only thus, Scaglione implies, can civilised life be made possible.[53] This initial over-reaction was then moderated by later writers, who benefited from Boccaccio's initial breakthrough in the sense that, once the basic point had been made so forcefully and the need to follow nature so firmly established, they were in the fortunate position (which Boccaccio was not) where they could afford to

[51] A. Scaglione, *Nature and Love in the late Middle Ages*, p. 68: '. . . the *Decameron* is, indeed, a conscious revolt against prevailing standards, as the Proem to the Fourth Day will show. Nor could the "balance" be restored without temporarily going overboard in the opposite direction. Briefly, the excesses of spiritualism had to be corrected by an outburst of naturalism.'

[52] *Ibid.*, p. 80: '. . . in Boccaccio's radical subjecting of all human faculties to the tyrannical, uncompromising rule of love, with impatient disregard of all constraints, be they individual (*senno*) or collective (social distinctions and conventions, morality itself), one can sense a certain potential "anarchism".'

[53] *Ibid.* See the chapter on 'Morality as conciliation between nature and society', especially p. 84: 'Compromises with the "conventions" of artificial organization are, then, inevitable, since nature (conceived as the mere obedience to primeval instincts) and society (the artificial order brought about by custom and "reason") are distinct and partly opposed realities.'

restore the balance, and qualify the excesses of his position, without compromising the fundamental doctrine of naturalism itself.

Although there is much truth in these observations, it seems to me that they present, as a whole, too exclusive a view. It is true that Boccaccio does understandably over-react in his desire to establish the satisfaction of natural desires as the only sensible basis of all human behaviour, and that as a result the indulgence of instinct in the stories of the *Decameron* is not always reconciled with the need to show consideration for others (it sometimes takes the form of a gratification of selfish desires that proves harmful to others, a fact that perhaps justifies Scaglione's comment that 'a touch of hypocrisy cannot be denied in this moral system').[54] But it is not, I think, correct to assume that Boccaccio is so extreme in his advocacy of naturalism that he loses sight of the need ultimately to temper natural instinct by the exercise of some form of control. Nor is it true that the only way he can envisage the application of such a moderating influence is through a tame acceptance of the unsatisfactory disicplines of the old order. Boccaccio is certainly no revolutionary. For all its shortcomings, he is prepared to accept the established order of society as a whole, as the necessary context of all eventual reform: witness his implicit respect of the law in the Introduction to Day I: ' "... le leggi, nelle solle citudini delle quali è il bene vivere d'ogni mortale, ..." '.[55] But this does not necessarily involve a tacit surrender of

[54] *Ibid.*, p. 89.
[55] *Decameron*, p. 30: ' "... the law, to whose care is entrusted the well-being of all men, ..." ' A similar formulation occurs in Day IX, story 9: '... le leggi, le quali il ben comune riguardano in tutte le cose, ...' (*Decameron*, p. 1081), where the respect is further extended to include usage and custom: '... e l'usanza o costume che vogliam dire, le cui forze son grandissime e reverende, ...' (*Decameron*, p. 1081). See the translation of the passage on p. 54 (note 86).

principle, for Boccaccio's re-evaluation of moral criteria calls for a radical reorganisation of the ethical sub-strata on which that society is based, a reorganisation which would be pursued within the existing framework of society but which would ultimately correct its current abuses and make it more humane, just and fair.

Such changes as these require the substitution of artificial disciplines by more natural and reasonable ones that are compatible with the legitimate satisfaction of natural instinct. And what has not perhaps been fully recognised is that in the *Decameron* Boccaccio is already feeling his way towards such a solution. He is beginning to envisage the establishment of a state of harmonious equilibrium between the satisfaction of instinct and the application of proper and reasonable restraint, whereby standards of virtue, responsibility and self-discipline can be upheld. In other words, he is already beginning to visualise reason as a guiding and controlling agent.

Although, in Boccaccio's eyes, all human behaviour is conditioned, and man is not, therefore, a completely free-willed being, it does not follow from this that he is simply a helpless and blameless victim of environmental forces. For he is not *just* a creature of instinct: he also possesses a conscious intellect, an individual will and a capacity for independent action, and hence (unlike the rest of the animal kingdom) he does have a sense of moral responsibility, and must ultimately be held accountable for his actions. In the Conclusion to Day IX Panfilo states that the acquisition of fame through the practice of virtue is something which ' "ciascuno che al ventre solamente, a guisa che le bestie fanno, non serve, dee non solamente desiderare, ma con ogni studio cercare e operare" '.[56] And

---

[56] *Decameron*, p. 1095. See the translation of the passage on p. 83 (note 135).

in the *Genealogie Deorum Gentilium Libri*[57] Boccaccio observes, 'Non quidem adeo ignarus sum, quin noverim liberi arbitrii, quo omnes valemus, potentia possimus nature superare vires; quod egisse non nullos legimus.'[58] Boccaccio here recognises the existence of free will and acknowledges that human behaviour is not *entirely* dictated by natural environmental forces.

So while nature and instinct are the primary realities on which all morality must be based, reason and intellect also have their part to play. The rational faculty too is something natural, given by God for man to make fullest and best possible use of. On the one hand this makes possible the pursuit of scholarship and culture (with beneficial moral effects), on the other the regulation of personal behaviour in everyday life. Although Boccaccio rejects the artificial forms of restraint which contemporary society sought to impose on natural behaviour, he is not, I think, advocating blind, reckless surrender to instinct, regardless of the consequences. Satisfaction of natural instinct must be allied to a measure of responsibility and consideration of others if it is to avoid causing distress or injury to one's fellows. Boccaccio counsels moderation, therefore, advocates prudence and discretion in following nature (and not solely for reasons of expediency). The difference is that the restraint he envisages would be a natural restraint, achieved through the exercise of the natural human faculty of reason; it implies the proper and responsible satisfaction of natural desires instead of the attempt to crush and subdue them.

What Boccaccio is proposing, therefore, albeit in a fragmentary, tentative and somewhat inconsistent fashion as yet, is natural rational control of natural irrational

---

[57] *Genealogie Deorum Gentilium Libri*, Bari, 1951: book xv, chapter 10.
[58] See the translation of the passage on p. 16 (note 29).

instinct, a moral ideal that would be a perfect balance of nature and reason, where the golden mean would be to follow nature reasonably, to secure a controlled satisfaction of natural appetite through the judicious application of the intellect, the enlightened use of reason, the liberal exercise of sound judgement and common sense. In this way reason can be employed to refine and elevate human behaviour, and to ensure the maintenance of civilised standards of conduct. It is our intellect that allows us to understand human nature, that enables us to step back and look at our behaviour from without, as Boccaccio has done. It makes for greater self-awareness and self-knowledge, the ability to be objective about ourselves, to see ourselves as others see us, to look critically at our own actions, to evaluate the motives, discern the causes and envisage the consequences of our behaviour; and this self-awareness makes, in turn, for moral responsibility, for the capacity for self-control and self-discipline, upon which all civilised conduct depends. This projected adherence to a norm of nature and reason, this sense of moderation and developing instinct for restraint are the logical moral counterparts of the classicism of the *Decameron* in the aesthetic sense; and as the latter reflects Boccaccio's maturity as a writer, so the former reflect his maturity as a man.

Boccaccio's use of the word *ragione* is revealing here. It is, as we would expect, applied to the use of reason in the regulation of human behaviour and the control of natural instincts: for example in the eighth story of Day X:

'Chi dunque, lasciando star la volontà e con ragion riguardando, più i vostri consigli commenderà che quegli del mio Gisippo?'[59]

[59] *Decameron*, p. 1180. ' "Who, then, putting wilfulness aside, and considering the matter reasonably, would think your advice more commendable than that of my friend Gisippus?" '

and again in Filomena's words in the Introduction to Day I:

'Ricordivi che noi siam tutte femine, e non ce n'ha niuna sì fanciulla, che non possa ben conoscere come le femine sieno ragionate insieme e senza la provedenza d'alcuno uomo si sappiano regolare.'[60]

But it also indicates the existence of a moral right, the personal prerogative which the enlightened use of the intellect establishes for the actions of the individual who allows himself to be so governed, as in Pampinea's remark in the Introduction to Day I:

'Donne mie care, voi potete, così come io, molte volte avere udito che a niuna persona fa ingiuria chi onestamente usa la sua ragione. Natural ragione è, di ciascuno che ci nasce, la sua vita, quanto può, aiutare e conservare e difendere.'[61]

The implication of such a statement is that the observance of reason in the direction of one's affairs constitutes the moral justification of a given course of action. Notice too how nature and reason appear to complement each other

[60] *Decameron*, pp. 34–5. '"Remember that we are all women, and none of us is so childish that she is not fully aware that women are not always guided by reason when they are together, and cannot organise their affairs properly without a man to supervise them."'

[61] *Decameron*, p. 29. '"My dear ladies, you will often have heard, as I have, that you harm no one by exercising your lawful rights. Every human being has a natural right to foster, preserve and defend his own life, as far as he is able."' For similar use of *ragione* with the force of *diritto* (moral right), see Day V, story 9 (*Decameron*, p. 675): '"... ed è ragione, per ciò che niuno altro diletto, niuno altro diporto, niuna consolazione lasciata t'ha la tua strema fortuna"'. '"... and it is right and proper, for your extreme misfortunes have left you no other delight, no other recreation, no other consolation."' Similarly in Day X, story 4 (*Decameron*, p. 1129); '... il primo signore niuna ragione avesse più nel suo servidore, ...' '... the first gentleman no longer had any right to his servant, ...' And again in Day X, story 8 (*Decameron*, p. 1182): '"... l'una è Sofronia tenendovi, nella quale, più che mi piaccia, alcuna ragion non avete"'. '"... firstly, you hold on to Sophronia, although you have no right to do so without my permission."'

here, as also in Boccaccio's own words to his lady readers in the Introduction to Day IV:

... per ciò che io conosco che altra cosa dir non potrà alcun con ragione, se non che gli altri e io, che vi amiamo, natural-mente operiamo.[62]

The identification is such, indeed, that *ragione* serves on occasion to designate the natural order itself, the estab-lished laws of creation, which are themselves the supreme expression of *divine* reason in the harmonious disposition of the universe as a whole:

'... gl'Iddii, li quali noi dobbiam credere che con ragion perpetua e senza alcuno errore dispongono e governan noi e le nostre cose.'[63]

The search for a balance between reason and nature as the answer to the problem of morality is nothing new. It is certainly not the brainchild of the Renaissance. Reason and nature, spirit and senses, mind and body, will and instinct, are two contrasting dimensions of all human experience, and each age seeks to effect its own compro-mise between them. In medieval experience, however, that compromise was all too often an impermanent and unstable one which manifested itself in an uneasy tension between warring extremes (Petrarch's inner conflicts, for instance) and achieved only a negative equilibrium, a precarious state in which two incompatible and essentially irreconcilable forces opposed each other, and cancelled each

[62] *Decameron*, p. 459. See the translation of the passage on pp. 29–30 (note 44). The same is true of Emilia's observations on the dependence of women on men (*Decameron*, Day IX, story 9, pp. 1080–1; see p. 54 above). It is, she holds, both natural and reasonable, part of the established order of things, the norm from which we should not seek to depart.

[63] Day X, story 8 (*Decameron*, pp. 1176–7). '"... the gods, who, we must believe, order and govern us and our affairs according to perfect and everlasting laws."' See also note 160 below.

other out in a kind of stalemate; or else the tension was resolved by the victory of the one over the other, resulting either in a thoughtless hedonism or in the exaltation of the mind at the expense of the body, the glorification of the spirit, and the corresponding mortification of the flesh, the ruthless subjugation of natural instinct. This latter solution was the one favoured by the medieval Church, which threw the full weight of its authority behind the forces of the mind, the spirit and the will (which, properly directed, it hailed as virtue) and condemned the surrender to the body and the senses as sin and vice.

Many Renaissance writers,[64] on the other hand, and Boccaccio too, aspired to effect a more harmonious balance. Nature and reason are seen as two differing but mutually compatible sides of human experience which together 'make the round', and which, given the right conditions, can coexist in a state of peaceful equilibrium. The satisfaction of natural instinct urged by Boccaccio in the *Decameron* is not intrinsically incompatible with *all* forms of moral restraint. What is indicated is rather that the restraint should be of an enlightened and reasonable kind that respects human instinct and meets its requirements instead of suppressing or frustrating them. The satisfaction of natural instinct is indeed so *far* from being incompatible with moral restraint that it is an essential condition of virtue, the prerequisite of all decent moral conduct.

---

[64] Ariosto, Montaigne, Chaucer (an early figure, like Boccaccio) and Shakespeare are some of the more obvious examples.

IX

VIRTUE AND FULFILMENT

Reasonable, responsible, controlled fulfilment of natural human needs is the foundation of Boccaccio's conception of virtue. To follow nature reasonably, indulging one's natural instincts moderately and prudently, leads not only to the observance of standards of propriety, decency and decorum, as in the case of the 'sobrie e oneste donne' of the *cornice*;[65] it leads also to a more natural and genuine form of altruism than the coercive exhortation to self-sacrifice of the medieval Church: one which results not merely from a sense of duty or moral obligation but from a spontaneous overflowing of the self, a superabundance of goodwill, a natural magnanimity and generosity of spirit, arising out of a feeling of fulfilment, plenitude and well-being, which in turn derives from the proper satisfaction of one's natural instincts. So the hallmark of natural, reasonable behaviour, the outward and visible signs of the controlled satisfaction of natural desires, are courtesy and consideration of others, respect for the rights and dignity of one's fellow man.

The virtues celebrated in the stories of the *Decameron* are almost all of this kind: magnanimity, generosity, liberality, courtesy, hospitality, fidelity, kindness and compassion (the selfless courtesy and hospitality of Federigo,[66] and the ready generosity of Cisti,[67] for instance). But the clearest illustrations are to be found in the stories of the

---

[65] Introduction to Day I (*Decameron*, p. 39); the word *onestà* in Boccaccio indicates decency and respectability; the word *virtù* often implies a more active and operative virtue, closer to altruism.

[66] Day V, story 9.   [67] Day VI, story 2.

tenth day. At the end of the *Decameron* we encounter conspicuous examples of virtue and nobility of spirit that are
in many ways the culmination of the entire work. Rational
self-control and moral responsibility occasion sublime instances of munificence: the compassion of King Piero,[68]
the gracious hospitality of Messer Torello,[69] the spectac-
ular forbearance of the faithful Griselda[70] (the supreme
embodiment of patience and virtue, whose story is a
fitting conclusion both to this series of tales and to the
Decameron as a whole). The mind is in control here,
ordering and directing natural impulses. Man is fulfilled,
composed, contented, overflowing with natural goodwill
to his fellows, made capable of supreme acts of altruism.
It is this consideration and respect for others, plus the
observance of standards of decency and decorum, that
makes possible that spirit of co-operation and concord,
that genuine sense of fellowship and community, which
are essential for the promotion of an ordered, civilised,
social existence, an existence of which respect for the law
is an essential part.[71] The social relations of the characters
in the *cornice* are a picture of the sort of social harmony
which Boccaccio envisages in this ideal state of society,
where everyone allows himself to be governed by reason
and nature, and where fulfilment and responsibility go
hand in hand.[72]

Such a conception of virtue remains, however, an individual rather than a collective one. True virtue is not
imposed from without: it comes from within the self. The
touchstone of moral conduct (as revealed in the reply of
Filomena to Neifile in the Introduction to Day I)[73] is a
clear conscience, not the opinion of others. If the individual feels in his heart that he has acted properly, that

[68] Day X, story 7.   [69] Day X, story 9.   [70] Day X, story 10.
[71] See p. 35.   [72] See chapters XIV and XV   [73] See chapter VI, p. 77.

is all that matters. Social convention is binding on him only when it has his own willing assent, and it is a necessary condition of that obedience to the laws which Boccaccio is so concerned to encourage that they should be just and reasonable, and calculated to foster a good state of society. The recognition of the need for restraint is maintained in the *Decameron*, but it is now a voluntary, natural, self-imposed restraint, not an alien discipline imposed arbitrarily from without. The important thing is to obey the dictates of one's own conscience, regardless of how one's behaviour may appear when judged by conventional standards of conduct.

Once again we can see reflected here the mature experience of the author himself. The spontaneous form of altruism which Boccaccio depicts for us in the *Decameron* is the same kind which he himself manifests in his statement of the aim of composition. In the *Proemio* he states that he intends to provide consolation, solace and distraction for women who are unhappy in love because they are frustrated in the fulfilment of their desires, and that he wishes to do so as a mark of gratitude for his own deliverance from the pangs of unrequited love. He is proposing, therefore, to assist those who are still enmeshed in the toils of an unhappy passion, to alleviate them in their distress and to help them obtain a measure of the relief and freedom he now enjoys. So here too we encounter a natural overflowing of goodness and humanity, of sympathy and compassion, in one who is composed, at peace with the world and with himself, and hence both able and willing to help others less fortunate than he to attain that state themselves.

It would seem to me, therefore, that Boccaccio has been done less than justice here. Anarchy is not just round the corner, as the society of the *cornice* shows. Far from

commending wayward and lawless behaviour, Boccaccio
is in fact advancing, in a tentative and experimental form,
the basis of a totally new kind of morally responsible conduct. The concept of the new control is not yet as fully or
as coherently articulated as the revolt against the old. The
formulation of moral criteria is still hesitant and pro-
visional, and the application is not always entirely con-
sistent. Boccaccio appears at times to sanction some forms
of self-indulgence that prove injurious to others, especially where love and the abuse of intelligence are concerned. There are specific cases where they threaten to
overcome all moral scruple, unreasonable or otherwise.[74]
But he is not prescribing heedless licence, thoughtless
hedonism and a complete disregard for others, whatever
inconsistencies there may be. His idea of the role of reason
as the guide and moderator of nature may not yet be
envisaged clearly enough to constitute a completely
autonomous system of ethics that would be proof against
all charges of immorality, egoism and sexual degeneracy:
this is one of the reasons for his retraction of the book in
later life, and his reversion to a more conventional and
ascetic kind of morality—the contemporary criticisms he
had affected to disclaim so lightly had bitten deeper than
at first appeared.[75] But, for all this, the harmonious
equilibrium established by later writers, between the satisfaction of natural instinct and the civilising forces of the
intellect and the rational will, is already anticipated in the
Decameron itself. Reason is already assuming here the
function it was to fulfil in the high Renaissance.

[74] See chapter x, p. 51, and note 83 below; and chapter xiii, p. 77, and
note 127 below.
[75] For a fuller discussion of this problem see note 37 above.

X

LOVE AND MARRIAGE

The general concept of morality that emerges from the *Decameron* as a whole (the recognition of the necessity of satisfying natural instinct, and the developing awareness of a corresponding need to temper its harmful excesses and to promote responsible, civilised behaviour by regulating human life according to reasonable criteria) finds specific expression in the treatment of a wide range of individual topics: love and marriage, the place of women in society, religion, intelligence, education and culture, courtesy, nobility and fortune. Each of these distinctive but interrelated themes is an integral part of the whole; each in its way constitutes an attempt to apply these general criteria to particular moral issues.

The principal natural instinct whose validity Boccaccio is concerned to assert is love. Love in the *Decameron* is not the idealised spiritual aspiration of medieval lyric poetry. It is not religious, transcendental or Platonic. It still at times retains the chivalrous overtones of courtly love, but it is nevertheless essentially a real human emotion, comprising, on the one hand, sexual attraction, erotic love, sensual and physical passion, and, on the other, personal feeling, tenderness, affection and devotion. And it is, as Boccaccio asserts in the Introduction to Day IV,[76] an essential part of the natural order of life. As such, there is nothing sinful or shameful about it: it is a normal, healthy impulse, in which it is quite right and proper to take a

[76] '. . . gli altri e io, che vi amiamo, naturalmente operiamo' (*Decameron*, p. 459). Boccaccio is addressing his lady readers. See the translation of the passage on pp. 29–30 (note 44).

wholehearted and unreserved delight.[77] This is Boccaccio's own argument in the Conclusion of the book, in reply to the charge of immorality: there is nothing wrong in these stories about love; love is part of the natural order, and is perfectly wholesome in itself; if it offends you it is because your own mind is sick. He compares it to wine, which is excellent for the healthy man, and injurious only to the sick; and to fire and weaponry, which are beneficial agents when rightly employed, and harmful or wrong only if abused:

Chi non sa ch'è il vino ottima cosa a' viventi, secondo Cinciglione e Scolaio e assai altri, e a colui che ha la febbre è nocivo? direm noi, per ciò che nuoce a' febbricitanti, che sia malvagio? Chi non sa che 'l fuoco è utilissimo, anzi necessario a' mortali? direm noi, per ciò che egli arde le case e le ville e le città, che sia malvagio? L'arme similmente la salute difendon di coloro che pacificamente di viver disiderano, e anche uccidon gli uomini molte volte, non per malizia di loro, ma di coloro che malvagiamente l'adoperano. Niuna corrotta mente intese mai sanamente parola: e così come le oneste a quella non giovano, così quelle, che tanto oneste non sono, la ben disposta non posson contaminare, se non come il loto i solari raggi o le terrene brutture le bellezze del cielo.[78]

Hence love in the *Decameron* is free from all sense of guilt,

[77] See the passage from Day VIII, story 7, already quoted on p. 27.

[78] *Decameron*, pp. 1240–1. 'We all know that wine is an excellent thing for healthy people, as Boozy and Toper and many others affirm, but that it is harmful to a man with a fever. Are we to call it evil because it harms the sick? We all know that fire is most useful, not to say indispensable, to mankind. Are we to call it evil because it burns down houses, villages and towns? Weapons, likewise, protect the welfare of those who wish to live in peace, and are often also the cause of men's death, not because they are wicked in themselves but because of the viciousness of those that use them. Foul minds never take any word in a wholesome sense; and just as a foul mind gains no benefit from decent words, so a healthy mind cannot be tainted by language that is somewhat less than decent, any more than mud can defile the sunlight or the filth of the earth can sully the beauty of the heavens.'

all qualms of conscience, all bigotry, hypocrisy and false modesty. It is a candid, frank and uninhibited emotion that expresses itself fully and freely, an irresistible force to which none of us is immune, and which therefore acknowledges none of the artificial restrictions and taboos which contemporary society sought to impose on it. It is, Boccaccio implies, both inevitable and right that love should violate and disregard social conventions whenever they attempt to deny the legitimate expression of that emotion.[79]

The greatest practical obstacle to the achievement of happiness in love is the medieval debasement of marriage as a result of sacrificing love to expediency. The arranged marriages of the Middle Ages sacrifice natural instincts and affections for the sake of securing political or financial advantages, and thus infidelity and adultery become inevitable as the patterns of natural instinct reassert themselves. Medieval marriage was usually mundane and practical, often degraded to the level of a business contract, a political and financial convenience. There was seldom much room for romance, and in such circumstances love frequently had to be sought elsewhere. Boccaccio seems to suggest that the unhappy wife is justified in taking a lover, provided she is discreet: hence the mockery of cuckolds, and the tacit approval of the action of their wives in deceiving them. Boccaccio displays here a liberal and permissive attitude to sex, but for all that he is not, I think, sanctioning unbridled licence and reckless indulgence in love. He is not a libertine, advocating indiscriminate free love and condoning all promiscuity and adultery, regardless of the circumstances. He urges moderation, tact and prudence (and not solely

[79] See the examples given in chapter III, pp. 12–15.

on grounds of convenience). He recognises the need for responsibility in love; and he does not criticise marriage as an institution, only the debasement of that institution in medieval society. Boccaccio respects marriage in itself, and, provided that it takes place by free choice and mutual consent, he regards marital fidelity as an important virtue. He praises the constancy of the good wife: it is no coincidence that the most outstanding example of virtue in the *Decameron* should be a wife's faithfulness to her husband (the story of Griselda).[80]

Marriage is seen as a two-way arrangement. The woman should be treated with consideration and understanding by the husband, and should be faithful in return. If the husband fails to satisfy the wife, and care for her properly, then he fails to fulfil his side of the bargain, and she is no longer morally bound to keep her part of the agreement. Her trust has been betrayed, her obligations removed, and she is justified in being unfaithful. Examples of infidelity resulting from bad marriages, where the wife has not been properly treated, occur in Day III (stories 4, 5 and 8), Day IV (story 10), Day V (story 10), and Day VII (stories 1, 5, 8 and 9). The cause of adultery is always the husband's failure to satisfy the wife; this may result from an arranged marriage, made without regard to love (Day V, story 10, and Day VII, story 8); it may be a consequence of the husband's ascetic outlook (Day III, story 4, and Day VII, story 1), or of his advanced age (Day III, story 4, Day IV, story 10, and Day VII, story 9); sometimes it is a product of his excessive jealousy and rigid confinement of his wife within doors (Day III, story 8, and Day VII, story 5), or of his greed and his willingness to exploit his wife's attractiveness for financial gain (Day III, story 5). The basic point that an ill-treated

[80] Day X, story 10.

wife is no longer bound by her marriage vows is made explicit in the tenth story of Day V:

> . . . lasciando il cattivo uomo con la mala ventura stare con la sua disonestà, . . . liete riderete degli amorosi inganni della sua donna, compassione avendo all'altrui sciagure, dove bisogna.[81]

And especially in the fifth story of Day VII:

> Nobilissime donne, la precedente novella mi tira a dovere io similmente ragionar d'un geloso, estimando che ciò che si fa loro dalle loro donne, e massimamente quando senza cagione ingelosiscono, esser ben fatto: e se ogni cosa avessero i componitori delle leggi guardata, giudico che in questo essi dovessero alle donne non altra pena avere constituta che essi constituirono a colui che alcuno offende sé difendendo; per ciò che i gelosi sono insidiatori della vita delle giovani donne e diligentissimi cercatori della lor morte. Esse stanno tutta la settimana rinchiuse e attendono alle bisogne familiari e domestiche, disiderando, come ciascun fa, d'aver poi il dì delle feste alcuna consolazione, alcuna quiete, e di potere alcun diporto pigliare, sì come prendono i lavoratori de' campi, gli artefici delle città e i reggitori delle corti, come fece Iddio che il dì settimo da tutte le sue fatiche si riposò, e come vogliono le leggi sante e le civili, le quali, allo onor di Dio e al ben comune di ciascun riguardando, hanno i dì delle fatiche distinti da quegli del riposo. Alla qual cosa fare niente i gelosi consentono, anzi quegli dì che a tutte l'altre son lieti, fanno ad esse, più serrate e più rinchiuse tenendole, esser più miseri e più dolenti: il che quanto e qual consumamento sia delle cattivelle quelle sole il sanno che l'hanno provato. Per che conchiudendo, ciò che una donna fa ad un marito geloso a torto, per certo non condennare ma commendare si dovrebbe.[82]

But prevention is better than cure, and one of Boccaccio's

[81] *Decameron*, p. 680. '. . . leaving the scoundrel to wallow unhappily in the consequences of his fault . . . you will laugh with glee at the amorous intrigues of his wife, taking pity on another's misfortunes where need be.'
[82] *Decameron*, pp. 806–7. 'Most noble ladies, the previous story prompts me to tell another tale about a jealous husband, as I consider that what

aims in writing the *Decameron*, as he intimates in the *Proemio*, is to secure a more natural and humane treatment of women in general. The reform of the institution of marriage would be a necessary part of such an aim, for marriage, properly used, is an indispensable condition of the kind of virtuous conduct which Boccaccio seeks to promote: virtue founded on responsible, controlled satisfaction of natural appetite. In its proper form it is a reasonable discipline that allows the full expression of love, while at the same time ensuring that consideration and respect for others on which civilised behaviour depends. Boccaccio *does*, therefore, envisage the need for rational control in love, even if that control is not always consistently applied in the stories themselves (where it is not, for instance, always clear that the husband has been at fault when the wife is adulterous).[83]

---

their wives do to them is right and proper, especially when they are jealous without cause. If the lawgivers had taken all things into account, in my judgement they should not have imposed on such a wife a punishment greater than that incurred by someone who injures another in self-defence; for jealous husbands are always laying traps for young wives, and seeking assiduously to encompass their downfall. They are cooped up all week long, attending to family and household chores, and on Sundays they wish, like everyone else, to have some rest, some solace and some recreation, just as farm labourers, town workers and magistrates do, as God himself did when he rested from all his labours on the seventh day, and as is decreed in the laws of Church and State, which, for the glory of God, and in the interests of public welfare, have separated working days from days of rest. But jealous husbands will have none of it; on the contrary, they make the days which are joyful for all other women even more gloomy and unhappy for their wives by keeping them more tightly locked up than ever. Only those poor souls who have had to bear such adversity can know how wearing it is. And so, to sum up, whatever a wife does to a husband who is jealous without cause should surely be applauded rather than condemned.'

[83] For example, Day III, story 7; Day IV, story 9; Day VI, story 7; Day VII, stories 2, 3, 6, 7 and 10; and Day VIII, stories 2 and 8.

XI

A WOMAN'S PLACE

The *Decameron* is, of course, written for women in love who are unhappy and frustrated in the fulfilment of their desires.[84] And the book is in a certain sense an apologia for women, an assertion of their rights as human beings, and a protest against the ill treatment and the under-privileged position of women in medieval society. To this extent it represents the start, however tentative, of female emancipation. Most medieval literature on the subject of women was influenced by the ascetic and anti-feminist sentiments of early religious writers like St Jerome. Woman was commonly regarded as the temptress of man, the embodiment of the sins of the flesh, and celibacy was seen as the only sure path to salvation. Attacks on women were a common theme of medieval satire. There were occasional defences of women, but nothing that amounted to much had appeared before Boccaccio's own time. There were, for example, an anonymous *Lode e biasimo delle donne*, and a *contrasto* by Antonio Pucci, a contemporary of Boccaccio's, who draws attention to the in-justices of the married state (though each of these two compositions mingles criticism with more favourable re-marks). There was, in addition, Francesco da Barberino's *Del Reggimento e costumi di donna*, which belongs to the early years of the fourteenth century (1309–15): the author's attitude to women is sympathetic and relatively free from prejudice, and he is prepared to allow young

[84] See the *Proemio* (*Decameron*, pp. 5–7) and also the Conclusion (p. 1243), where it is repeated that the stories are 'scritte per cacciar la malinconia delle femine', '. . . written to dispel the melancholy of women.'

girls a certain limited freedom of social activity, but he still accepts the domestic confinement of women as a necessary fact of life once the age of marriage approaches (Boccaccio is well in advance of this position in the *Decameron*). Finally there are other works of a similar but more popular nature, consisting of advice to young wives, and written in much the same spirit.

In medieval society the status of women was, of course, vastly inferior to that of men. Women were thought, in fact, to be inferior beings, closer to the animal state (whence the notion that they were more lusty and passionate than men). They were not credited with the same intelligence as men; were not, on the whole, thought capable of learning and culture. Their role in society was either functional and menial (as mother and housewife), or else purely decorative (as a pretty social ornament). At the same time there also existed the chivalrous and literary tradition of courtly love, and the idealisation of woman as the vehicle of divine grace, and the embodiment of perfect virtue, in the medieval lyric convention. But this did not materially affect the actual position of women in society. The *madonna* may have seemed a remote goddess to the poet who worshipped her from afar, but her position in relation to her husband was still one of humble subservience, for all her noble birth.

Boccaccio's liberal attitudes bring him in the *Decameron* to criticise the injustice of this state of affairs. He is *not* yet advocating the equality of the sexes: he considers that women should submit to the authority of men. Elissa bears this out in the Introduction to Day I when she says:

'Veramente gli uomini sono delle femine capo, e senza l'ordine loro rade volte riesce alcuna nostra opera a laudevole fine.'[85]

[85] *Decameron*, p. 35. '"Truly, men are our masters, and without their guidance it is seldom that any of our enterprises is brought to a worthy

and this statement is confirmed by Emilia's remarks in the ninth story of Day IX:

Amabili donne, se con sana mente sarà riguardato l'ordine delle cose, assai leggiermente si conoscerà tutta la universal moltitudine delle femine dalla natura e da' costumi e dalle leggi essere agli uomini sottomessa, e secondo la discrezion di quegli convenirsi reggere e governare; e per ciò ciascuna che quiete, consolazione e riposo vuole con quegli uomini avere a' quali s'appartiene, dee essere umile, paziente e ubidente, oltre all'essere onesta: il che è sommo e spezial tesoro di ciascuna savia. E quando a questo le leggi, le quali il ben comune riguardano in tutte le cose, non ci ammaestrassono, e l'usanza o costume che vogliam dire, le cui forze son grandissime e reverende, la natura assai apertamente cel mostra, la quale ci ha fatte ne' corpi dilicate e morbide, negli animi timide e paurose, nelle menti benigne e pietose, e hacci date le corporali forze leggieri, le voci piacevoli, e i movimenti de' membri soavi: cose tutte testificanti noi avere dell'altrui governo bisogno. E chi ha bisogno d'essere aiutato e governato, ogni ragion vuol lui dovere essere obediente e subietto e reverente all'aiutatore e al governator suo: e cui abbiam noi aiutatori e governatori, se non gli uomini? Dunque agli uomini dobbiamo, sommamente onorandogli, soggiacere; e qual da questo si parte, estimo che degnissima sia non solamente di riprension grave, ma d'aspro gastigamento.[86]

This, for Boccaccio, is a natural state of affairs: it is part of the natural order of things that the husband should be the

---

conclusion."' The observation is made in response to an expression of similar sentiments by Filomena (see p. 39 above).

[86] *Decameron,* pp. 1080–1. 'Sweet ladies, if you observe the order of things with a sound mind you will recognise with the greatest of ease that our entire sex has been made subject to men by nature, by custom and by law, and that it is for us to be managed and governed according to men's good sense. So every woman who wishes to live in peace, solace and repose with the men to whom she belongs must be modest, patient and obedient, as well as virtuous: wherefore every wise woman prizes these gifts, and makes them her own. And even if these things were not taught us by the law, which seeks in all things to promote the common good, and by usage,

dominant partner. He did indeed still believe man to be both the mental and physical superior of woman, as can be seen in the *De claris mulieribus*. A woman's place is still principally the home, her proper role one of dutiful and obedient submission to the authority of a considerate and loving husband, father or brother.

But Boccaccio sees that women are not just part of men's goods and chattels. They are not just beasts of burden, unpaid domestic servants, and the physical means of producing heirs; nor are they merely decorative ornaments. They are intelligent human beings [87] and deserve

---

or custom as we call it, whose powers are mighty and sacred, they are still made unmistakably clear to us by nature, who has given us soft and delicate bodies, meek and timorous spirits, a mild and kindly disposition, and has endowed us with but slight strength of frame, with sweet voices and gently moving limbs: all of which indicates that we need others to guide us. And those who need help and guidance must, by all that is just and reasonable, respect and humbly obey those who help and guide them: and whom have we to help and guide us if not our menfolk? Therefore we must submit to men, and do them great honour; and any woman who does not follow this course to my mind deserves not only severe reproof but harsh punishment.'

[87] The stories of Day VII in particular substantiate this assertion: the tricks which women play on their husbands in these tales are intended to illustrate their intelligence and resourcefulness. See especially Day VII, story 2 (*Decameron*, pp. 783-4): 'Carissime donne mie, elle son tante le beffe che gli uomini vi fanno, e spezialmente i mariti, che, quando alcuna volta avviene che donna niuna alcuna al marito ne faccia, voi non dovreste solamente esser contente che ciò fosse avvenuto o di risaperlo o d'udirlo dire ad alcuno, ma il dovreste voi medesime andare dicendo per tutto, acciò che per gli uomini si conosca che, se essi sanno, e le donne d'altra parte anche sanno: il che altro che utile essere non vi può, per ciò che, quando alcun sa che altri sappia, egli non si mette troppo leggiermente a volerlo ingannare. Chi dubita dunque che ciò che oggi intorno a questa materia diremo, essendo risaputo dagli uomini, non fosse lor grandissima cagione di raffrenamento al beffarvi, conoscendo che voi similmente, volendo, ne sapreste fare? È adunque mia intenzion di dirvi ciò che una giovinetta, quantunque di bassa condizione fosse, quasi in un momento di tempo, per salvezza di sé, al marito facesse.' 'My dearest ladies, men play so many tricks on you—and husbands more than most—that, on those occasions when a wife plays one on her husband, you should not only be pleased when you learn of it, or are told of it by others, but you should tell people all about it yourselves, so that men may realise that they are not the only ones who are smart. If you

to be treated as such. Men should not ignore them, shut them away, and leave them to vegetate in a world of exclusively domestic trivia: such restrictions are both unreasonable and unnatural. Boccaccio is therefore opposed to the cruelty of rigid domestic confinement, the custom of keeping women pent up in private chambers, and causing them frustration, distress and boredom, an unenviable plight which he describes with obvious sympathy in the *Proemio*:

E chi negherà, questo [conforto], quantunque egli si sia, non molto più alle vaghe donne che agli uomini convenirsi donare? Esse dentro a' dilicati petti, temendo e vergognando, tengono l'amorose fiamme nascose, le quali quanto più di forza abbian che le palesi coloro il sanno che l'hanno provato e provano; e oltre a ciò, ristrette da' voleri, da' piaceri, da' comandamenti de' padri, delle madri, de' fratelli e de' mariti, il più del tempo nel piccolo circuito delle loro camere racchiuse dimorano, e quasi oziose sedendosi, volendo e non volendo in una medesima ora, seco rivolgono diversi pensieri, li quali non è possibile che sempre sieno allegri. E se per quegli alcuna malinconia, mossa da focoso disio, sopravviene nelle lor menti, in quelle

---

do, you will surely profit by it, since, when one person knows another is clever, he does not try so readily to deceive him. Who, then, would doubt that if the things which we shall say on the matter today were known to all men they would be a very strong deterrent to them in their deceptions, as they would realise that you could, if you wished, beat them at their own game? For this reason I intend to tell you of the trick that a young woman, though of humble extraction, played on her husband on the spur of the moment, to save herself from discovery.' But similar stories occur on other days too: the tenth story of Day V, for instance (see p. 50), and the fourth story of Day VIII: '. . . intendo di dirvene una [novella] d'un proposto, il quale, malgrado di tutto il mondo, voleva che una gentil donna vedova gli volesse bene, o volesse ella o no: la quale, sì come molto savia, il trattò sì come egli era degno.' (*Decameron*, p. 906.) '. . . I intend to tell you the story of how a rector, regardless of what the world might think, was bent on making love to a widowed lady of gentle birth, whether she liked it or not; and of how she, wise woman that she was, treated him as he deserved.'

conviene che con grave noia si dimori, se da nuovi ragionamenti non è rimossa: senza che elle sono molto men forti che
gli uomini a sostenere; il che degli innamorati uomini non
avviene, sì come noi possiamo apertamente vedere. Essi, se
alcuna malinconia o gravezza di pensieri gli affligge, hanno
molti modi da alleggiare o da passar quello; per ciò che a loro,
volendo essi, non manca l'andare attorno, udire e veder
molte cose, uccellare, cacciare, pescare, cavalcare, giucare o
mercatare.[88]

Women should rather, he implies, be allowed to exercise
their minds in cultural pursuits and in intelligent conversation, like the ladies in the *cornice*, a point which Pampinea forcibly substantiates in the tenth story of Day I:

Valorose giovani, come ne' lucidi sereni sono le stelle
ornamento del cielo e nella primavera i fiori de' verdi
prati, così de' laudevoli costumi e de' ragionamenti piacevoli
sono i leggiadri motti. Li quali, per ciò che brievi sono,
molto meglio alle donne stanno che agli uomini, in quanto
più alle donne che agli uomini il molto parlare e lungo,
quando senza esso si possa fare, si disdice, come che oggi
pocheo niuna donna rimasa ci sia la quale o ne 'ntenda alcuno

[88] *Decameron*, pp. 5–6. 'And who would deny that this comfort, whether
great or small, is more properly due to gentle ladies than to men? Women,
in fear and shame, keep the flames of love hidden within their tender
breasts, and how much stronger such fires are when they are concealed
those who have felt them, and who feel them still, know well; and what is
more, restricted as they are by the will, the wishes and the orders of
fathers, mothers, brothers and husbands, they spend most of their
time pent within the narrow confines of their rooms, and, sitting as if
in idleness, are prey to conflicting desires, and meditate on many things
which cannot possibly all be cheerful. And if in the course of such thoughts
their minds are invaded by a melancholy born of the fires of longing,
there to their great distress it must dwell, unless it is dispelled by other
preoccupations; besides which, they are not as strong as men are to bear
these things. Men who are in love are not affected thus, as we can plainly
see. They have many ways of alleviating or removing such melancholy
or gloomy thoughts as may afflict them, for they may, if they wish, walk
abroad, hear and see many things, go out fowling, hunting, fishing, riding
and gaming, or else engage in commerce.' He returns to the charge in the
introduction to the fifth story of Day VII (see p. 50).

leggiadro o a quello, se pur lo 'ntendesse, sappia rispondere: general vergogna e di noi e di tutte quelle che vivono. Per ciò che quella virtù che già fu nell'anime delle passate hanno le moderne rivolta in ornamenti del corpo; e colei la quale si vede indosso li panni più screziati e più vergati e con più fregi, si crede dovere essere da molto più tenuta e più che l'altre onorata, non pensando che, se fosse chi addosso o in dosso gliele ponesse, uno asino ne porterebbe troppo più che alcuna di loro; né perciò più da onorar sarebbe che uno asino. Io mi vergogno di dirlo, per ciò che contro all'altre non posso dire che io contro a me non dica: queste così fregiate, così dipinte, così screziate, o come statue di marmo mutole e insensibili stanno o sì rispondono, se sono addomandate, che molto sarebbe meglio l'avere taciuto; e fannosi a credere che' da purità d'animo proceda il non saper tra le donne e co' valenti uomini favellare, e alla loro milensaggine hanno posto nome onestà, quasi niuna donna onesta sia se non colei che con la fante o con la lavandaia o con la sua fornaia favella: il che se la natura avesse voluto, come elle si fanno a credere, per altro modo loro avrebbe limitato il cinguettare.[89]

The Conclusion to Day III, where Neifile neatly rebuffs Filostrato's quip, provides indeed a concrete example of

[89] *Decameron*, pp. 111–12. 'Worthy young ladies, as the stars adorn the clear night sky, and spring flowers the green meadows, so are good manners and pleasant discussion enhanced by the niceties of wit; and these, by virtue of their brevity, are much better suited to ladies than to gentlemen, as great and lengthy discourse is less becoming to women, when it can be avoided, than it is to men. Yet nowadays there are scarcely any women left who can even understand a witticism, let alone make an apt rejoinder, which is a shameful indictment of all our sex today. For this ability of mind possessed by the ladies of the past has been replaced in modern women by physical adornment, and the woman who observes that her clothes are more ornate, more gaudily striped and richer in colours than the rest thinks she should be more greatly honoured, and held in higher esteem than the others, not thinking that if anyone were to dress an ass in them, or just to pile them on its back, it could bear a great deal more than any of them, nor would it merit any more praise for that than asses usually do. I am ashamed to say it, for I cannot condemn others without standing condemned myself, but these bedecked, painted, multi-coloured women either stand there dumb and senseless, like marble statues, or, if asked a question, make the sort of reply that would be

the degree of wit and conversational repartee that women can display, if encouraged to use their natural intelligence in this way; and further instances occur in the stories.[90] The educated and articulate young ladies of the *cornice* are, in fact, the natural forebears of the cultured and accomplished *donne di palazzo* of the *Cortegiano*.

These ideas of Boccaccio's can be seen to anticipate the arguments of other Italian writers in much later times: Castiglione in the Renaissance, and Parini in the Enlightenment, for instance. It is yet another sign of the modernity of his outlook. However great the distance in time and the difference in attitude between the medieval Boccaccio and the militant suffragettes of the nineteenth and twentieth centuries (and they are both, of course, considerable), it is perhaps not altogether impossible to envisage a line of descent that would link the one to the other. The point of view here advanced is not final or definitive, however. Boccaccio's attitude to this question, and to many others, underwent considerable revision in later life as he retreated to more conservative positions.[91] The early humanists (of whom Petrarch, and later Boccaccio, were the most articulate and influential) were not, on the whole, very progressive in this respect. They still held the view that celibacy was best, and maintained that women and marriage were distractions from scholarship and study. In the *Corbaccio*, a typically medieval satire on

---

better left unsaid; and they persuade themselves that their inability to converse with ladies and gentlemen stems from innocence, and they call their stupidity virtue, as if the only decent women are those who speak just to the maid, and the washerwoman, and the baker's wife: whereas if nature had intended this, as they so fondly believe, she would have found other ways of restricting their chatter.'

[90] See Day I, stories 5 and 9; Day VI, stories 3 and 7, and Day VIII, story 2. The repartee that brings Day III to its close is on p. 440 of the *Decameron*.

[91] See note 37 above.

women, Boccaccio regresses from the relatively enlightened stand of the *Decameron* to an anti-feminist attitude in
keeping with traditional medieval and early humanist
thinking. The *Corbaccio* is a vigorous attack on women,
and a praise of celibacy as the only proper adjunct to the
life of the true scholar. This sudden and substantial reversal of attitude is only partly explained by Boccaccio's
dogmatic espousal of the humanist creed after his meeting
with Petrarch in 1351: it is conceivable that he was also
embittered by some particularly unhappy experience in
love. However this may be, the progressive approach to
women set out in the *Decameron* must be seen only as an
expression of the sympathetic sentiments of Boccaccio's
earlier years.

XII

RELIGION: A CRITICAL VIEW

Boccaccio's criticisms of the medieval Church and his denunciation of the clergy need to be interpreted with care. First, it should be observed that they are part of a well established medieval tradition, a large measure of which emanated from within the Church itself, from practising laymen like Dante, from popular preachers and monastic orders (the early Franciscan movement, the later 'spiritual Franciscans', St Catherine of Siena and her followers), and from learned and influential clerics of Boccaccio's own day, such as Petrarch. Next, we should bear in mind that Boccaccio's contribution too may come from this quarter. We know that he became a cleric, and it is at least possible that he was already a priest when he was writing the *Decameron* in the 1340s.

If he was, it would of course add a new perspective to his criticisms of the clergy. However, it is not known with certainty when he entered holy orders. Billanovich[92] has established that in 1360 Boccaccio was entrusted by Innocent VI with the care of souls in a cathedral church, a responsibility which suggests that he had then already been in holy orders for some time. Billanovich also makes the point that Boccaccio, like Petrarch, never married, and that all his children (at least five) were therefore illegitimate. This fact is of course most easily explained by assuming that Boccaccio was bound from a comparatively early age by the vow of celibacy, possibly even from his youth, when his father set him to study

[92] G. Billanovich, *Restauri Boccacceschi*, Edizioni di *Storia e Letteratura*, Rome, 1947.

canon law in Naples. But against all this must be set his habit, in the *Decameron*, of referring to the clergy as 'they' (without a suggestion that he himself was connected with the Church), the freedom with which he discusses his own experience of love, and the frank admission, in the Introduction to Day IV, not only that he finds sex a delightful activity but that his pursuit of it is entirely legitimate:

Dicono adunque alquanti de' miei riprensori che io fo male, o giovani donne, troppo ingegnandomi di piacervi, e che voi troppo piacete a me. Le quali cose io apertissimamente confesso, cioè che voi mi piacete e che io m'ingegno di piacere a voi: e domandogli se di questo essi si maravigliano, riguardando, lasciamo stare l'aver conosciuti gli amorosi basciari e i piacevoli abbracciari e i congiugnimenti dilettevoli che di voi, dolcissime donne, sovente si prendono, ma solamente ad aver veduto e veder continuamente gli ornati costumi e la vaga bellezza e l'ornata leggiadria e oltre a ciò la vostra donnesca onestà; quando colui che nudrito, allevato, accresciuto sopra un monte salvatico e solitario, infra li termini di una piccola cella, senza altra compagnia che del padre, come vi vide, sole da lui disiderate foste, sole addomandate, sole con l'affezion seguitate. Riprenderannomi, morderannomi, lacerrannomi costoro se io, il corpo del quale il Ciel produsse tutto atto ad amarvi e io dalla mia puerizia l'anima vi disposi sentendo la virtù della luce degli occhi vostri, la soavità delle parole melliflue e la fiamma accesa da' pietosi sospiri, se voi mi piacete o se io di piacervi m'ingegno, e spezialmente guardando che voi prima che altro piaceste ad un romitello, ad un giovinetto senza sentimento, anzi ad uno animal salvatico? Per certo chi non v'ama e da voi non disidera d'essere amato, sì come persona che i piaceri né la virtù della naturale affezione né sente né conosce, così mi ripiglia, e io poco me ne curo.[93]

[93] *Decameron*, pp. 455–6. 'Now several of my critics say, young ladies, that I am wrong to try so hard to please you, and that I am too fond of you. All of which I openly admit: I *am* fond of you, and I do try to please

The existing evidence is inconclusive, and the case un-proved either way. The most reasonable hypothesis would perhaps be that Boccaccio took holy orders at the time he was made to study canon law, but was never com-mitted to the Church, and soon lost all interest. There-after, despite his disenchantment with ecclesiastical af-fairs, he would still be bound by his vow of celibacy, and with the change of attitude that occurred in later life he would then be in a position to take up the priesthood in earnest.

However this may be, it must be said that at the time of writing the *Decameron* his devotion to religion falls far short of what might be expected of a man called to the ministry. Throughout the book he appears, in strong contrast to Dante, as one who assents intellectually to Christianity but whose life is not dominated by his faith, and whose attitudes are not determined by the fervour of his convictions. His Christianity is at present dormant within him, not an active force in his personality, and he

---

you; and I would ask them why they find this surprising, considering how often I have seen, and still see, your gracious manners, your beauty and charm, your elegance and loveliness, and, moreover, your ladylike modesty, to say nothing of having known the loving kisses, the pleasur-able embraces and the delectable comminglings that you so often bestow upon us, my sweetest ladies; and seeing that one who was nurtured, raised and bred on a wild and lonely mountain, within the confines of a narrow cell, and with only his father for company, no sooner saw you than he desired only you, asked only for you, yearned only for you. Can my enemies still reprove, censure and condemn me if I find you pleasing, and seek in turn to please you, when heaven made my body specifically to love you, and I from my early youth gave my whole being to that end, feeling the power of your gaze, the sweetness of your gentle words, and the flame that is kindled by your tender sighs; especially as a young hermit, a witless youth, almost a wild animal in fact, liked you more than anything else he had known? Clearly, those who reprimand me thus neither love you, nor desire to be loved by you, because they neither know nor feel the pleasure or the power of natural affection, and so I pay them no heed.' The other principal statement to this effect, also from the Introduction to Day IV, is quoted on pp. 29-30.

does not yet seem to have thought long or deeply about the substance of his religious beliefs. Indeed, it is perhaps in part because he has not felt compelled to wrestle with the problems of theology and dogma that his conscience remains as yet unclouded by remorse, as he openly disowns the traditional moral teachings of the Church. His later history suggests that, when the crisis came, his liberal allegiances were not ultimately strong enough to protect him from the Church's powerful psychological weapons of guilt and fear.[94]

Certainly none of the earlier works in the vernacular (including the *Decameron*) is imbued with the active presence of the Christian faith. Clearly, he is still not greatly concerned with religion, and his main preoccupations lie elsewhere.[95] In the *Amorosa Visione* and the *Ninfale d'Ameto*, where Boccaccio still feels the need to pay lip service to the traditional morality of the medieval Church, the contradiction between the expressed ascetic ideal and the blatantly mundane and sensual interests of the author would strike the reader as mere hypocrisy, were the effects not so unintentionally comical. In the *Decameron*, where Boccaccio rejects the ascetic side of medieval Christianity, there is no longer any contradiction between the author's professed religious beliefs and his moral views: his own misgivings, subsequently so manifest, and possibly even inherent at the time of writing, can be more properly attributed to the conditioning effects of his education and upbringing, in the very religious and moral climate he sought to transcend, than to any serious inconsistency in his intellectual and moral position. However, Boccaccio's respect for religion in the *Decameron*, though genuine in itself, is still largely conventional.

[94] See p. 24 and note 37 above.
[95] See chapter VI.

The acknowledgement made by the story-tellers towards the Church and religion is predominantly formal and external, and at times even verges on the perfunctory.[96]

Thus if Boccaccio *was* a cleric from his early Naples days it would not be because he was a priest by vocation but because the priesthood in the Middle Ages (and for a long time thereafter) was the obvious profession for aspiring scholars like Petrarch and himself. Ecclesiastical training and academic scholarship frequently went hand in hand, and it was by no means unusual for the scholar to be bound by religious vows. The Church provided him with education, financial security and the leisure and seclusion to pursue his studies undisturbed. The clergy consequently played a significant part in the development of the humanist movement, and celibacy, as we have observed,[97] was commonly regarded by the early humanists as a desirable condition, since it left the scholar free to concentrate on his work.

But whatever reservations we may have about the strength of Boccaccio's convictions, or the extent of his commitment, we can at least be sure, in the light of the evidence, that his religious objections are not those of a godless rebel and libertine consciously rejecting the Christian faith and its institutions. Traditional religious values and beliefs are not the anchors of his life at this stage, nor the criteria on which his view of life is founded. But he was never opposed to religion as such, and the charge of disrespect of religion brought against him by his contemporaries, to which he replies in the Conclusion

[96] For their pious reaction to the story of Ser Ciappelletto see p. 66 below. The explanation is that Boccaccio cannot repress his sneaking admiration for Ciappelletto's intelligence, despite his recognition that such behaviour is morally wrong.

[97] See p. 59.

blameworthy

Unorthodox with others

of the book,[98] is essentially unfounded. He was throughout his life an orthodox Christian who never challenged
the substance of the Christian faith; and this orthodoxy is
reflected in the *Decameron*, despite his relative indifference
to such matters at the time. Impiety is received with conventional expressions of disapproval, as in the case of Ser
Ciappelletto's amusing but reprehensible profanation of
the sacrament in making a false confession before receiving
extreme unction: '. . . egli era il piggiore uomo forse che
mai nascesse';[99] '. . . dico costui più tosto dovere essere
nelle mani del diavolo in perdizione che in paradiso';[100]
and the narrators are scrupulous in their observance of
religious practices, breaking off their entertainments at
weekends to attend to their devotions. At the end of Day
II Neifile says:

'Come voi sapete, domane è venerdì e il seguente dì sabato,
giorni, per le vivande le quali s'usano in quegli, alquanto
tediosi alle più genti; senza che 'l venerdì, avendo riguardo
che in esso Colui che per la nostra vita morì sostenne passione,

[98] 'E chi starà in pensiero che di quelle ancor non si truovino che
diranno che io abbia mala lingua e velenosa, per ciò che in alcun luogo
scrivo il ver de' frati? A queste che così diranno si vuol perdonare, per
ciò che non è da credere che altro che giusta cagione le muova, per ciò che
i frati son buone persone e fuggono il disagio per l'amor di Dio, e maci-
nano a raccolta e nol ridicono; e se non che di tutti un poco viene del
caprino, troppo sarebbe più piacevole il piato loro.' (*Decameron*, p. 1244.)
'And who would suppose that there will not be some among you who
will say that I have an evil and poisonous tongue because in one or
two places I have written the truth about the friars? Those who say
this are to be forgiven, for we should not imagine that they do not
have just cause, as the friars are good people who shun discomfort
for the love of God, and who do their grinding only on the full flood,
and never breathe a word. And if it was not for the fact that they all
stink a bit of old goat it would be extremely pleasurable to consort with
them.' Boccaccio here reaffirms the truth of his criticisms of the clergy
under the guise of irony.
[99] *Decameron*, Day I, story 1, p. 50. '. . . he was perhaps the worst man
ever born.'
[100] *Decameron*, p. 65. '. . . I say a man like that should be in the clutches
of the devil in hell rather than in heaven.'

è degno di reverenza; per che giusta cosa e molto onesta reputerei che, ad onor d'Iddio, più tosto ad orazioni che a novelle vacassimo. E il sabato appresso usanza è delle donne di lavarsi la testa e di tor via ogni polvere, ogni sucidume che per la fatica di tutta la passata settimana sopravvenuta fosse; e sogliono similmente assai, a reverenza della Vergine Madre del Figliuol di Dio, digiunare, e da indi in avanti per onor della sopravvegnente domenica da ciascuna opera riposarsi: per che, non potendo così appieno in quel dì l'ordine da noi preso nel vivere seguitare, similmente stimo sia ben fatto, quel dì delle novelle ci posiamo.'[101]

This suggestion meets general agreement, and so:

... li due dì seguenti a quelle cose vacando che prima la reina aveva ragionate, con disiderio aspettarono la domenica.[102]

Similar arrangements are made for the second weekend, at the end of Day VII:

Ma poi che la sua canzon fu finita, ricordandosi la reina che il dì seguente era venerdì, così a tutti piacevolmente disse: 'Voi sapete, nobili donne e voi giovani, che domane è quel dì che alla passione del nostro Signore è consecrato, il quale, se ben vi ricorda, noi divotamente celebrammo, essendo reina Neifile, e a' ragionamenti dilettevoli demmo luogo; e il simigliante

---

[101] *Decameron*, p. 307. '"As you know, tomorrow is Friday, and the day after, Saturday, days that are rather irksome to most folk because of the sort of food we normally eat during them. Furthermore Friday is sacred to the Passion of Our Lord, who died that we might live. And so I should consider it most right and proper that for the glory of God we should devote it to prayer rather than to stories. And on the Saturday women usually wash their hair, and remove from their persons all the dust and dirt of the week's labours. Moreover, many people are accustomed to observe a fast as a mark of respect for the Virgin Mother of the Son of God, and from then on to rest from all labour in honour of the approaching sabbath. Wherefore, as we shall be unable to follow fully the routine we have established on that day either, I consider it proper for us to abstain once more from story-telling."'

[102] *Decameron*, p. 310. '... devoting the next two days to those things to which the queen had earlier referred, they looked forward eagerly to Sunday.'

facemmo del sabato susseguente. Per che, volendo il buono essemplo datone da Neifile seguitare, estimo che onesta cosa sia che domane e l'altro dì, come i passati giorni facemmo, dal nostro dilettevole novellare ci asteniamo, quello a memoria riducendoci che in così fatti giorni per la salute delle nostre anime addivenne.'[103]

And on the following Sunday they go to church:

Già nella sommità de' più alti monti apparivano, la domenica mattina, i raggi della surgente luce, e ogni ombra partitasi, manifestamente le cose si conosceano, quando la reina levatasi con la sua compagnia primieramente alquanto su per le rugiadose erbette andarono, e poi in su la mezza terza una chiesetta lor vicina visitata, in quella il divino officio ascoltarono.[104]

What Boccaccio *is* opposed to, in the *Decameron* at least, is <u>asceticism</u> and the corruption of the clergy. He may accept the conventional teaching of the Church in matters of faith, but on the question of morals he prefers to exercise independent judgement. To a great extent, of course, he still embraces Christian moral standards: charity, pity, mercy, altruism—all have a high place in his scheme of values. But he is not, at *this* stage in his life, prepared to accept the rigid austerity of medieval morality

---

[103] *Decameron*, p. 870-1. 'But when her song was finished the queen recalled that the following day was Friday, so she said pleasantly to everyone, "You know, young men and noble ladies, that tomorrow is the day that is sacred to the Passion of Our Lord, and, if you remember, when Neifile was queen we devoutly observed it, and called a halt to our agreeable discussions; and we did the same on the following Saturday. So, as I wish to follow the good example set by Neifile, I consider it the proper thing to abstain from telling these enjoyable stories of ours during tomorrow and the next day, just as we did last week, and to meditate on that which was done on those days for the salvation of our souls."'

[104] *Decameron*, p. 875. 'The light of the rising sun was already appearing amid the highest mountain peaks on Sunday morning, all the shadows had departed, and everything was clearly visible, when the queen and her companions rose, walked first for a while over the dewy grass, and then, about half past seven, visited a nearby chapel, where they heard divine service.'

or the ascetic religious values upon which it largely re-sided.[105] The clergy are seen as ordinary fallible mortals beneath the cowl, human beings like the rest of us, with the same instincts and the same weaknesses, subject to the laws of nature like everyone else. Not only their con-gregations but they themselves are unable to act according to the values to which they subscribe. Inevitably they cannot practise what they preach, and succumb to the very temptations which they so earnestly enjoin others to resist. They break their vows because they are forced to, because they cannot help themselves. This is especially clear in the case of the vows of chastity and celibacy, as the story of Masetto and the nuns makes plain.[106] And the consequences of this failure are, as always in such circum-stances, hypocrisy, false piety and dissimulation, all of which is amply illustrated in the numerous stories of promiscuity and subterfuge in which the clergy figure so prominently.[107] The clergy's attempt to deny their own sexual instincts is a parallel to the enforced chastity of women before marriage, with the difference that their discipline is usually voluntary and self-imposed, though even this distinction does not apply in cases where men and women have been obliged by others to take up a monastic life to which they did not feel themselves called.

As we would expect, Boccaccio reveals considerable sympathy and indulgence whenever the misdemeanours of the clergy are simply caused by human weakness, by the inability to resist natural instinct.[108] Provided there is no distress caused to others, he does not condemn. But when

[105] For Boccaccio's reversal of this position in later life, and the causes thereof, see note 37 above.

[106] Day III, story 1. See the passage quoted on p. 13.

[107] See Day I, stories 2, 4 and 6; Day III, stories 1, 4, 8 and 10; Day IV, story 2; Day VI, story 10; Day VII, story 3; Day VIII, story 2, and Day IX, story 2.

[108] See Day I, story 4; Day III, stories 1 and 10, and Day IX, story 2.

the bigotry, the deceit and corruption are deliberate and calculated he often takes a different view. When the clergy are *using* religion as a cloak for the conscious furtherance of their selfish desires (to obtain alms by false pretences or to gratify their lust), when they are taking unscrupulous advantage of their position of privilege in society to exploit their fellows and to play upon the superstition and credulity of their congregations, when they are in control of their actions, and indifferent to the effects of their fraudulent and criminal behaviour on others, then Boccaccio speaks out against them, both personally and through his narrators, as, for example, in the seventh story of Day I:

La viziosa e lorda vita de' cherici, in molte cose quasi di cattività fermo segno, senza troppa difficultà dà di sé da parlare, da mordere e da riprendere a ciascuno che ciò disidera di fare.[109]

The speaker here is Filostrato. Further instances of explicit criticisms of this sort occur in the following passages:

. . . essi, il più stoltissimi e uomini di nuove maniere e costumi, si credono più che gli altri in ogni cosa valere e sapere, dove essi di gran lunga sono da molto meno, sì come quegli che per viltà d'animo non avendo argomento, come gli altri uomini, di civanzarsi, si rifuggono dove aver possano da mangiar, come il porco . . .[110]

---

[109] *Decameron*, p. 96. 'The foul and corrupt life of the clergy, which through its wickedness presents us in many ways with a clear target, has little difficulty in providing material for discussion, criticism and reproof to all who wish to engage in such.'

[110] *Decameron*, Day III, story 3, pp. 336–7. '. . . though they are for the most part totally obtuse, and men of outlandish manners and habits, they think themselves worthier and wiser in all matters than other people are, whereas they are far inferior, and resemble those who are too spineless to fend for themselves like other men, and who lodge themselves, like pigs, wherever they can find food . . .'

Usano i volgari un così fatto proverbio: 'Chi è reo e buono è tenuto, può fare il male e non è creduto'; il quale ampia materia a ciò che m'è stato proposto mi presta di favellare, e ancora a dimostrare quanta e quale sia la ipocresia de' religiosi, li quali co' panni larghi e lunghi e co' visi artificialmente pallidi e con le voci umili e mansuete nel domandar l'altrui, e altissime e rubeste in mordere negli altri li loro medesimi vizi e nel mostrare sé per torre e altri per lor donare venire a salvazione; e oltre a ciò, non come uomini che il Paradiso abbiano a procacciare come noi, ma quasi come possessori e signori di quello, danti a ciaschedun che muore, secondo la quantità de' danari loro lasciata da lui, più e meno eccellente luogo; con questo prima se medesimi, se così credono, e poscia coloro che in ciò alle loro parole dan fede, sforzandosi d'ingannare. De' quali, se quanto si convenisse fosse licito a me di mostrare tosto dichiarerei a molti semplici quello che nelle lor cappe larghissime tengon nascoso.[111]

Ma che dico io di frate Rinaldo nostro, di cui parliamo? Quali son quegli che così non facciano? Ahi vitupero del guasto mondo! Essi non si vergognano d'apparir grassi, d'apparir coloriti nel viso, d'apparir morbidi ne' vestimenti e in tutte le cose loro, e non come colombi ma come galli tronfi con la cresta levata pettoruti procedono: e che è peggio (lasciamo stare d'aver le lor celle piene d'alberelli di lattovari

[111] *Decameron*, Day IV, story 2, pp. 478–9. 'The common people have a saying: ' "A man who is wicked and thought to be good, can sin without people believing he would." This proverb furnishes me with ample material for a story on the theme prescribed, and also to show you the nature and extent of the hypocrisy of the monks and friars, whose robes are long and ample, whose faces are made artificially pale, whose voices are meek and humble when they beg for alms but loud and imperious when decrying in others the vices of which they themselves are guilty, and in showing that their path to salvation is through greed and that of others through charity towards them; and what is more, they act not as do men who must strive to attain paradise, like the rest of us, but as if they were its lords and masters, assigning to every man that dies a more or less exalted place, according to the amount of money he has left them. And in this way they strive first to delude themselves, if they actually believe what they say, and then to deceive those who give credence to them. And if I were allowed to tell what should be told, I would soon reveal to many gullible folk what they conceal beneath their capacious cloaks.'

e d'unguenti colmi, di scatole di vari confetti piene, d'ampolle
e di guastadette con acque lavorate e con oli, di bottacci di
malvagia e di greco e d'altri vini preziosissimi traboccanti,
intanto che non celle di frati ma botteghe di speziali o d'un-
guentari appaiono più tosto a' riguardanti) essi non si vergognano che altri sappia loro esser gottosi, e credonsi che altri
non conosca e sappia che i digiuni assai, le vivande grosse e
poche e il viver sobriamente faccia gli uomini magri e sottili e
il più sani; e se pure infermi ne fanno, non almeno di gotte
gl'infermano, alle quali si suole per medicina dare la castità
e ogni altra cosa a vita di modesto frate appartenente. E
credonsi che altri non conosca, oltra la sottil vita, le vigilie
lunghe, l'orare e il disciplinarsi dover gli uomini pallidi e
afflitti rendere, e che né San Domenico né San Francesco,
senza aver quattro cappe per uno, non di tintillani né d'altri
panni gentili ma di lana grossa fatti e di natural colore, a
cacciare il freddo e non ad apparere si vestissero. Alle quali cose
Iddio provegga, come all'anime de' semplici che gli nutricano
fa bisogno.[112]

---

[112] *Decameron*, Day VII, story 3, pp. 792-3. 'But why do I speak only of
this friar Rinaldo of ours? Which of the friars does *not* behave thus?
Curse of this rotten world that they are! They feel no shame when seen
to be fat, to have painted cheeks, to wear soft materials, and to have such
dainty ways. And yet they are not dovelike, but flaunt themselves like
strutting cocks, with crest raised high and chest thrown out. Their cells are
full of jars of creams and ointments; there are boxes stuffed with various
sweets, phials and bottles of oils and specially prepared liquids, flasks
brimful of malmsey, Greek wine and other fine rare wines, so that they do
not appear to the onlooker like friars' cells at all but more like the shops
of apothecaries or perfumers. But let us pass over all this, for there is
worse to come. They do not blush when it is known that they have gout,
and suppose that others do not know full well that constant fasting, a plain
and frugal diet, and a life of continence keep men lean and thin, and healthy
for the most part; and if they do fall ill, it is not with gout at any rate, as
the normal cure for gout is abstinence, and everything else that is proper to
the life of a humble friar. And they suppose that others do not realise that,
in addition to sparse fare and prolonged fasting, prayer and strict discipline
ought to make men pale and drawn, and that neither St Dominic nor St
Francis had four cloaks each, but wore coarse, untreated woollen habits to
keep out the cold, not dyed fabrics and other fine clothes for show. We
need God to look to such matters, and to have a care for the simple souls
who provide the friars with sustenance.'

Belle donne, a me occorre di dire una novelletta contro a
coloro li quali continuamente n'offendono senza poter da noi
del pari essere offesi, cioè contro a' preti, li quali sopra le
nostre mogli hanno bandita la croce, e par loro non altramenti aver guadagnato il perdono di colpa e di pena, quando
una se ne possono metter sotto, che se d'Alessandria avessero
il soldano menato legato a Vignone.[113]

. . . con ciò sia cosa che essi tutti avarissimi troppo più che le
femine sieno, e d'ogni liberalità nimici a spada tratta: e quantunque ogn'uomo naturalmente appetisca vendetta delle
ricevute offese, i cherici, come si vede, quantunque la pazienzia
predichino e sommamente la remission delle offese commen-
dino, più focosamente che gli altri uomini a quella di-
scorrono.[114]

And the remarks made by Boccaccio in the Conclusion[115]
are the final manifestation of such sentiments. The
strength of feeling apparent in these statements is
occasioned by the sight of the clergy prostituting the
powers of the intellect, and perverting the faculty that
should be the source of a reasonable and natural kind of
virtue to a gratification of self at others' expense irrespective of the injuries it causes.

[113] *Decameron*, Day VIII, story 2, p. 881. 'Fair ladies, I must tell you a
tale that attacks those who do us constant wrong without our being able
to return the compliment. I mean the priests, who tilt at our wives with
crusading zeal, and when they manage to lay one of them out they think
they have earned as much pardon and remission of sin as if they had
dragged the sultan in chains from Alexandria to Avignon.'

[114] *Decameron*, Day X, story 2, p. 1106. '. . . since they are all far greedier
than we women ever are, and sworn enemies of all forms of generosity;
and though any man naturally yearns to gain revenge for the wrongs he has
suffered, the clergy, as we see, pursue their vengeance with a greater
ardour than others do; and yet they preach meekness, and roundly applaud
the forgiveness of injuries.'

[115] See note 98 above. The other major passage of forthright castigation,
excluded here because of its length, occurs in the seventh story of Day III,
pp. 387–90.

XIII

THE CELEBRATION OF INTELLIGENCE

It is in the same general context that we must view the
celebration of intelligence in the *Decameron*. Boccaccio
employs many words to describe different kinds of intelligence,[116] but he is not always discriminating in his
use of them,[117] and their meanings overlap to a certain
degree.[118] So it would appear wisest to attempt to define
the types of intelligence celebrated in the *Decameron* not
primarily according to the criterion of the words used to
describe them but rather on the basis of an empirical examination of the subject-matter of the tales. The principal

[116] *Ragione* designates the use of the intellect, or rational faculty in
general, to control natural instinct. It also means 'reasonableness' and
'rightfulness', qualities deriving from the enlightened use of these
reasoning faculties in the conscious and proper direction of the will
(see chapter VIII, pp. 38–40). *Ingegno* and *senno* usually refer to active,
operative intelligence, resourcefulness and ingenuity: *ingegno* in fact
frequently means a ruse, trick or stratagem. It may, however, also refer to
wit and repartee. *Sapere* indicates 'know-how', ability, expertise. *Sagacità*
indicates care, caution, circumspection and deliberation. *Saviezza* usually
means reflective wisdom (in Scaglione's words, it 'consists of being able to
understand the world and accept it as it is'), but it is also used in the sense
of *discrezione* (see below). *Discrezione* signifies discretion, but also discernment, perspicacity. *Avvedimento* may mean a number of things: shrewdness, perspicacity and discernment; resourcefulness and ingenuity; or an
expedient, ruse or stratagem.

[117] Compare the similarly casual list of alternative names for the
short story as a literary form in the *Proemio*: '. . . intendo di raccontare
cento novelle, o favole o parabole o istorie che dire le vogliamo, . . .'
(*Decameron*, p. 6). '. . . I intend to tell a hundred tales, or fables, or parables,
or stories, call them what you will, . . .'

[118] For instance, *ingegno*, which refers to both 'wittiness' and resourcefulness; *saviezza*, which can also mean discretion and discernment, like
discrezione; and *avvedimento*, which can signify perspicacity and discernment
(like *discrezione*), or resourcefulness and ingenuity (like *ingegno* and *senno*),
or a trick or stratagem (again like *ingegno*).

manifestations of intelligence that Boccaccio admires in his stories are as follows.

(1) Wit and repartee: neat replies, apt rejoinders, and the ability to make interesting conversation and to participate in stimulating discussion. This can be seen from the Introduction to the tenth story of Day I:

> Valorose giovani, come ne' lucidi sereni sono le stelle ornamento del cielo e nella primavera i fiori de' verdi prati, così de' laudevoli costumi e de' ragionamenti piacevoli sono i leggiadri motti.[119]

It may also be seen in the story of the marchioness of Monferrato, which begins with the approving observation of Fiammetta:

> . . . mi piace noi essere entrati a dimostrare con le novelle quanta sia la forza delle belle e pronte risposte, . . .[120]

It is especially clear in the stories of Day VI, as the proposal of the subject for that day indicates.[121] The best example is perhaps the witty reply of Cisti the baker to the servant who requested too much wine.[122] Finally, the narrators of the *cornice* furnish further examples of this kind of intelligence as they exercise their minds in lively debate and in witty conversational exchanges.[123]

(2) Calm, sober, reflective wisdom; the sanity, equanimity and equilibrium of the fulfilled and responsible man; profound understanding allied to serenity of spirit (the wisdom of Melchisedech in the third story of Day I, of Solomon in the ninth story of Day IX, and of Boccaccio himself in the *Proemio*).

---

[119] *Decameron*, p. 111. See the translation of the passage on pp. 57–8 (note 89).

[120] *Decameron*, Day I, story 5, p. 86. '. . . I am glad that we have begun to show in our stories how effective a swift and apt riposte can be, . . .'

[121] See note 158 below.

[122] *Decameron*, Day VI, story 2, pp. 710–11.

[123] See the Conclusion to Day III (*Decameron*, p. 440).

(3) Active, operative intelligence: resourcefulness and ingenuity, shrewdness, cunning, craft and guile (the resourcefulness of Masetto and the nuns in the first story of Day III, and of Fra Cipolla with the coals in the tenth story of Day VI).[124]

It is this last aspect of intelligence, as presented in the *Decameron*, that has previously received, perhaps, more emphasis than any other: intelligence as an expedient, and as an aid to the satisfaction of natural instinct, especially love. Clearly, intelligence *is* often envisaged principally as an ally and adjunct of nature that is designed to serve its ends. But there is more to Boccaccio's celebration of intelligence than this. The predominantly selfish application of intelligence is only one side, and not the most significant at that. The more important reason for the celebration of intelligence in the *Decameron* is that virtue itself cannot exist without it. For not only is intelligence able to secure the satisfaction of natural desires, it is in addition the only thing that makes possible the rational control of natural instinct, the regulation of violent passion, and the education and refinement of instinct and impulse that are the basis of all virtuous and responsible conduct, as we see from those tales where the right use of intelligence leads directly to virtuous behaviour.[125] It is, indeed, a

---

[124] Boccaccio usually employs *ingegno* for (i), *saviezza* for (ii), and *ingegno*, *senno*, or *avvedimento* for (iii). Of the other terms, *ragione* could, of course, apply to all three (but is seldom in fact used in so specific a sense when referred to intelligence); *discrezione* may apply to either (ii) or (iii); *sagacità* may apply to any of the three; *sapere* is more appropriate to (iii) than to the others. But *all* these identifications remain approximate only, for the reasons stated.

[125] For example, Day I, story 3 (Melchisedech and Saladin), story 5 (the Marchioness of Monferrato and the King of France), story 7 (Bergamino and Can Grande), story 8 (Guiglielmo Borsiere and Ermino de' Grimaldi), story 9 (the Gascon lady and the King of Cyprus), and story 10 (Alberto da Bologna and the lady who sought to shame him); Day VI, story 2 (Cisti and the servant), and story 3 (Monna Nonna de' Pulci and the Bishop of Florence); and Day X, story 10 (Griselda).

natural human faculty, given by God in part for this very purpose. This is not to say, of course, that Boccaccio has no other reasons for celebrating intelligence. He sees, for instance, that it is man's only real defence against ill fortune.[126] Furthermore a great deal of his enthusiasm is simply the result of a natural admiration of intelligence by a man who is highly intelligent himself and who does not suffer fools gladly. All manifestations of cleverness, astuteness and mental agility, of lively, nimble wits and alert, active, quick-witted minds command his instinctive respect. And his own native genius and somewhat impulsive nature mean that he has little patience with fools, dullards, simpletons and idiots, with those who are seen to be particularly superstitious, gullible or ignorant. One can sense the limits of Boccaccio's tolerance here. There is perhaps already a hint in this of the intellectual 'exclusiveness' of the early humanists, of that attitude of scholarly élitism and scorn for the common people that Boccaccio later strove (always rather unconvincingly) to assimilate from Petrarch.

This natural admiration of intelligence is such that, at times, Boccaccio even apparently condones slyness, trickery and deceit on the strength of it. He is prepared on occasion to view unscrupulous actions indulgently if the perpetrator has nimble wits, and even thoroughgoing rogues and thieves may command his respect when they are clever and resourceful. He evinces a sneaking admiration of their intelligence and expresses gentle but forthright ridicule of the stupidity of their dupes and victims (especially the foolishness of cuckolds, and the religious awe of the common people who swell the credulous congregations of the clergy).[127] This is not, however, because

126 See chapter XVI.
127 For Boccaccio's admiration of clever rogues see especially Day I,

Boccaccio regards intelligence as an *a priori* exemption from all moral sanction, as his stringent criticisms of the clergy indicate. It is, I think, because for the intelligent criminal some hope of moral redemption exists (as in the parallel case of Antonio and Sebastian in *The Tempest*). His intelligence has been perverted to crime but the potential for good is still there, and would indeed be realised if that intelligence could only be properly directed to virtuous ends, redirected from the selfish and unprincipled exploitation of his fellow men, to which it is at present harnessed, towards self-restraint and hence to the consideration of others. The clever rogue has sufficient intelligence to be fully conscious of the motives and consequences of his actions. He already has, therefore, the sort of self-awareness essential for the development of a proper sense of moral responsibility. And if at present he has deliberately chosen to flout moral standards, and to indulge his own selfish desires without regard to others, there is always the possibility of reorientation and reform. The case of the intelligent criminal thus reveals the essential difference between intelligence and reason as Boccaccio portrays them: intelligence is the innate potential of the natural faculty itself; reason is the right use of that faculty.

The stupid man, on the other hand, has, in Boccaccio's eyes, little chance of ever becoming truly virtuous—simply because he lacks the necessary intelligence. He is not clever enough to develop a sense of moral responsibility because he remains unable properly to envisage the

story 1 (Ciappelletto), which is discussed on p. 25, on p. 66, and in note 96 above; Day II, story 5 (Andreuccio and the Sicilian woman); Day IV, story 2 (Fra Alberto and Monna Lisetta); Day VI, story 10 (Fra Cipolla and the coals). For his mockery of fools see especially Day III, story 6 (Filippello's wife) and story 8 (Ferondo); Day VI, story 10 (Fra Cipolla's congregation), and Day VIII, story 3 (Calandrino).

causes and effects of his own actions, and hence is incapable of controlling them. A striking example of this kind of behaviour is given in the first of the Calandrino stories.[128] Calandrino is incensed because he supposes his wife to have brought all his toil to naught by breaking the spell of the heliotrope that made him 'invisible', and he vents his frustration on her by giving her a severe beating. This blind rage, and the act of senseless brutality in which it finds expression, are thus the direct product of his own stupidity. Such behaviour remains closer to that of animals: immediate, unthinking, instinctive indulgence of natural appetite (the Shakespearian parallel here is Caliban). Like that of animals, this type of conduct too is essentially amoral: there is behind it no proper sense of right and wrong. It is therefore innocent of criminal malice; but it is also by the same token devoid of all potential for virtue. For the intelligent immoral criminal some hope exists. For the innocent amoral fool there is none. So although the clever rogue is the more reprehensible of the two, because his anti-social behaviour is conscious, calculated and deliberate, whereas the uncivilised conduct of the fool is not, Boccaccio's sympathies nevertheless inevitably tend towards the former rather than the latter.

[128] Day VIII, story 3.

XIV

EDUCATION AND CULTURE

Intelligence, then, is the foundation of all virtue. But in order to realise its full potential for good it must first be educated and informed, so that it may be put to proper and beneficial uses, for if merely left to itself it can all too easily be diverted to the furtherance of criminal designs. Hence the admiration of intelligence in the *Decameron* logically culminates in the praise of education and culture: the activities and surroundings of the narrators in particular epitomise this educative process, and provide an eloquent tribute to its civilising power. The social graces and courtly accomplishments of the young men and women are not just window-dressing. Their cultured pursuits and pastimes,[129] in graceful and beautiful surroundings,[130] are all part of the elevation of human nature, and the refinement of human conduct, through the exercise of reason and the intellect. The narrators are training their aesthetic and intellectual capabilities, heightening their appreciation of beauty and knowledge, developing their sense of taste and their powers of discrimination and discernment: all of which, in Boccaccio's

[129] Singing, dancing, playing musical instruments, reciting poetry, playing chess, eating and drinking of the best, practising the art of witty and engaging conversation, taking part in intelligent and salutary discussions, telling entertaining and instructive stories, going for walks in the gardens of the villas and excursions in the surrounding countryside (to the *Valle delle Donne*, for instance).

[130] The charm of the Tuscan countryside, and the beauty of the villas and their gardens, whose tasteful and studied elegance (the beauty of nature enhanced by human art) provides us with a further instance of an ideal marriage of nature and reason in which the latter complements and perfects the former.

eyes, helps to promote virtue and to establish an ordered, civilised state of society. This is the humanist idea of education and culture ennobling the mind and inspiring virtue again. Notice the close parallel between the narrators, improving in knowledge, wisdom and virtue from their various cultural pursuits, and the humanist scholar, who achieves a similar effect through classical scholarship and the study of the literature of antiquity. In both, intelligence leads, through education, to knowledge and understanding, and thus to wisdom and virtue. Notice too that the narrators choose a secluded rural retreat, an echo of the humanist predilection for scholastic seclusion (Boccaccio at Certaldo, and Petrarch at Vaucluse).

The principal medium through which this education is provided, the main cultural agent for the diffusion of moral values among the young men and women of the *cornice*, is of course the telling of the stories themselves and the instructive discussion and debate that arise from this activity, in the course of which various kinds of motive, action and behaviour are considered, analysed and evaluated, and definite standards and values emerge.[131] By this means the story-tellers exercise their wits,[132] improve their minds, enrich their knowledge of human nature; progress as a consequence in virtue and nobility, in decency and decorum, in prudence and propriety, in courtesy and consideration; and establish as a result the harmonious social relations of an ideal state of society, as the narrators themselves are not slow to point out. In the Conclusion to Day VI Dioneo declares:

'Oltre a questo la nostra brigata, dal primo dì infino a questa

[131] For the origins, development and cultural significance of these social activities, and the extent to which they are reflected in Boccaccio's work, see the appendix.

[132] See chapter XIII, p. 75, and note 123 above.

ora stata onestissima, per cosa che detta ci si sia non mi pare
che in atto alcuno si sia maculata né si maculerà con lo aiuto
di Dio. Appresso, chi è colui che non conosca la vostra onestà?
la quale non che i ragionamenti sollazzevoli, ma il terrore della
morte non credo che potesse smagare.'[133]

And Panfilo reiterates these sentiments in the Conclusion
to Day X:

'. . . niuno atto, niuna parola, niuna cosa né dalla vostra parte
né dalla nostra ci ho conosciuta da biasimare: continua
onestà, continua concordia, continua fraternal dimestichezza
mi ci è paruta vedere e sentire.'[134]

This educative process reaches its climax in the telling of
the stories of the last day, where all compete in a spirit of
friendly rivalry, striving to outdo one another in narrating
tales of conspicuous virtue and altruism. The salutary
effects of such an occupation are emphasised in Panfilo's
proposal of the subject of these stories at the end of the
ninth day:

'. . . e per ciò voglio che domane ciascuna di voi pensi di
ragionare sopra questo, cioè: di chi liberalmente ovvero
magnificamente alcuna cosa operasse intorno a' fatti d'amore
o d'altra cosa. Queste cose e dicendo e udendo senza dubbio
niuno gli animi vostri ben disposti a valorosamente adoperare
accenderà: ché la vita vostra, che altro che brieve esser non
puote nel mortal corpo, si perpetuerà nella laudevole fama;

---

[133] *Decameron*, pp. 762–3. '"Moreover, this company of ours has
behaved impeccably from first to last. Nothing that we may have said
has cast a stain upon our behaviour, and so, with God's help, it shall
continue. Besides, your virtue is well known to all, and I do not think
that even the fear of death could shake it, let alone our entertaining
discussions."'

[134] *Decameron*, pp. 1234–5. '". . . I have seen nothing, in word, in deed
or in any other respect, for us to reproach ourselves with, either in your
conduct or in our own. I have, I think, both felt and seen continual
virtue, unbroken harmony, constant fellowship and concord."'

il che ciascuno che al ventre solamente, a guisa che le bestie fanno, non serve, dee non solamente desiderare, ma con ogni studio cercare e operare.'[135]

[135] Conclusion to Day IX (*Decameron*, pp. 1094-5). "'... and so want you all to think of a tale to tell tomorrow on the following theme: those who have behaved generously or magnanimously in love or in other matters. By hearing and telling these things you will without doubt inspire yourselves to perform worthy deeds, for which you are already prepared in spirit. In this way you will live on in fame and praise long after your mortal life, which cannot but be short, is done; and this is an aim that all those who are not enslaved like beasts to the belly should not merely wish for but should with the utmost zeal pursue and realise.'"

XV

COURTESY AND NOBILITY

A similar coherence informs Boccaccio's celebration of courtesy and nobility to that already observed in his praise of intelligence and culture. Courtesy and consideration are the hallmark of natural reasonable behaviour, the foundation of that spirit of friendship and co-operation upon which good society depends. Courtesy in Boccaccio thus comprises not only the more familiar and conventional chivalrous qualities of gallantry, gentility, politeness, civility, good manners and breeding (associated with the code of courtly love) but also the higher virtues exemplified in the stories of the last day.[136] In other words, it can be equated with altruism in the widest sense. Again this ideal of courteous behaviour is reflected in the conduct of the characters in the *cornice*. They live in concord with one another, accepting the benevolent rule of the king or queen of the day (further evidence that respect for the law, and the observance of reasonable convention, are an integral part of Boccaccio's conception of society). It is interesting to note in this respect how the relations between the narrators improve as the days go by, and the beneficial effects of their cultural activities become increasingly evident. To begin with there is some uneasiness and embarrassment, especially on the part of the ladies, and also occasional friction. In Day IV, story 2, for instance, Pampinea decides she will tell an amusing tale,

[136] See chapter IX, pp. 42–3; the principal virtues thus extolled are magnanimity, liberality, munificence, hospitality, fidelity, kindness and compassion (the first four of which embody the *nobler* aspirations of the chivalrous code of ethics).

and not just one which illustrates the moral theme chosen by Filostrato. Filostrato asks her to recount a sober, inspiring tale of tragic love, but Pampinea

... a sé sentendo il comandamento venuto, più per la sua affezione cognobbe l'animo delle compagne che quello del re per le sue parole, e per ciò, più disposta a dovere alquanto recrear loro che a dovere, fuori che del comandamento solo, il re contentare, a dire una novella, senza uscir del proposto, da ridere si dispose, e cominciò:[137]

Filostrato takes umbrage at this and scolds her:

Filostrato, udita la fine del novellar di Pampinea, sovra se stesso alquanto stette e poi disse verso di lei: 'Un poco di buono e che mi piacque fu nella fine della vostra novella; ma troppo più vi fu innanzi a quella da ridere, il che avrei voluto che stato non vi fosse.'[138]

But gradually these minor problems are resolved, and by the end of their stay in the country they have achieved the state of perfect harmony described by Panfilo in the Conclusion to Day X.[139]

Similar considerations determine Boccaccio's attitude to nobility. The acquisition of responsibility and virtue through natural, reasonable behaviour is the only standard by which it can be assessed. Man attains to true dignity of soul through the responsible satisfaction of natural instinct, which in turn leaves him fulfilled, whole in himself

[137] *Decameron*, p. 478. '... seeing that it was her turn, sensed instinctively the mood of the other ladies, and so, heeding that, rather than the wishes expressed by the king, and feeling it more her duty to entertain them somewhat than to satisfy him, except by keeping to the letter of his command, she decided to tell an amusing story without actually wandering from the subject, and she began thus:'

[138] *Decameron*, p. 494. 'Filostrato, having heard the end of Pampinea's tale, brooded for a while, and then said to her, "There was some virtue in the conclusion of your tale, and that pleased me; but before that there was far too much to laugh at, and I would rather you had left it out."'

[139] See p. 82. For examples of courtesy and consideration from the *stories* see chapter IX, pp. 42–3.

D

and capable of devoting his attention to the well-being of others. His criteria for nobility are thus intelligence, education, culture, courtesy and consideration. Human nature is *ennobled* as it develops in civilisation and culture through the proper education of the intellect—a further reflection of Boccaccio's humanist belief in the nobility of the intellect and the ennobling effects of culture and scholarship. This image transcends the feudal conception of nobility as an aristocracy based on birth and rank. It is independent of all considerations of ancestry, lineage and inherited social privilege, which are dismissed as mere accidents of fortune (and which are thus artificial criteria with no proper basis in natural merit). At the same time, Boccaccio's conception of nobility also rejects the bourgeois criterion of wealth. Nobility to Boccaccio is a question not of class or money but of *character*. It is essentially a spiritual thing. True nobility, like true virtue (for it is the same thing), dwells within the self and cannot be conferred or withdrawn by the external forces of the social order. It is therefore to be found in the poor and low-born as well as in the rich and aristocratic.[140]

The protagonists of the *novelle* provide ample evidence of the truth of this assertion. Guiscardo, for instance, as Ghismonda tells Tancredi, possesses true nobility, for all his poverty and humble birth:

'Di che egli pare, oltre allo amorosamente aver peccato, che

[140] Partly as a consequence of this belief (but partly also as a simple reflection of his own social background, or of the social provenance of a particular tale), the aristocracy is commonly portrayed by Boccaccio in the everyday circumstances of life, practically indistinguishable from the mercantile middle classes. Ricciardo and Caterina, for example, in the fourth story of Day V, have the modes and behaviour of the bourgeoisie. And even when something of the aristocratic honour remains in the actual conduct of the nobility (as in the chivalry of Federigo degli Alberighi in Day V, story 9) the setting and atmosphere are still predominantly middle-class Florentine.

tu, più la volgare oppinione che la verità seguitando, con più amaritudine mi riprenda, dicendo, quasi turbato esser non ti dovessi se io nobile uomo avessi a questo eletto, che io con uom di bassa condizione mi son posta: in che non ti accorgi che non il mio peccato ma quello della fortuna riprendi, la quale assai sovente li non degni ad alto leva, abbasso lasciando i dignissimi. Ma lasciamo or questo, e riguarda alquanto a' principi delle cose: tu vedrai noi d'una massa di carne tutti la carne avere, e da uno medesimo Creatore tutte l'anime con iguali forze, con iguali potenzie, con iguali virtù create. La virtù primieramente noi, che tutti nascemmo e nasciamo iguali, ne distinse; e quegli che di lei maggior parte avevano e adoperavano nobili furon detti, e il rimanente rimase non nobile. E benché contraria usanza poi abbia questa legge nascosa, ella non è ancor tolta via né guasta dalla natura né da' buon costumi; e per ciò colui che virtuosamente adopera, apertamente si mostra gentile, e chi altramenti il chiama, non colui che è chiamato ma colui che chiama commette difetto. Raguarda tra tutti i tuoi nobili uomini e esamina la lor vita, i lor costumi e le loro maniere, e d'altra parte quelle di Guiscardo raguarda: se tu vorrai senza animosità giudicare, tu dirai lui nobilissimo e questi tuoi nobili tutti esser villani. Delle virtù e del valore di Guiscardo io non credetti al giudicio d'alcuna altra persona che a quello delle tue parole e de' miei occhi. Chi il commendò mai tanto, quanto tu 'l commendavi in tutte quelle cose laudevoli che valoroso uomo dee essere commendato? e certo non a torto; ché se i miei occhi non m'ingannarono, niuna laude da te data gli fu che io lui operarla, e più mirabilmente che le tue parole non potevano esprimere, non vedessi: e se pure in ciò alcuno inganno ricevuto avessi, da te sarei stata ingannata. Dirai dunque che io con uomo di bassa condizione mi sia posta? tu non dirai il vero: ma per avventura, se tu dicessi con povero, con tua vergogna si potrebbe concedere, che così hai saputo un valente uomo tuo servidore mettere in buono stato; ma la povertà non toglie gentilezza ad alcuno, ma sì avere. Molti re, molti gran principi furon già poveri, e molti di quegli che la terra zappano e guardan le pecore già ricchissimi furono e sonne.'[141]

Love is here shown to be the great leveller. It abolishes all social distinctions and privileges. All start equal before it. Hence a considerate lover like Guiscardo is noble, whereas Tancredi's uncouth and ill mannered noblemen are not. Similarly Coppo di Borghese Domenichi, who is mentioned in the preamble to the ninth story of Day V, shows

[141] Day IV, story 1 (Decameron, pp. 470–2). "'And so it seems that you are not content to upbraid me for taking a lover, but that, paying more heed to a common fallacy than to the truth, you reproach me even more bitterly for consorting with a man of low estate, as you put it, as though you would not have been at all distressed if I had chosen to associate with a nobleman. In so doing you fail to notice that it is not my misdeed that you are condemning, but that of fortune, which very often raises the unworthy to a high eminence and leaves the worthiest men in lowly places. But let us now pass on from this, and pay some attention to first principles: you will then see that we are all created of the same flesh, and that our souls are all fashioned by the same Creator, with equal abilities, faculties and powers. We were all born equal, then, and still are, but what first distinguished us one from another was merit; and those who had a greater portion of it, and used it, were called noble, and the rest were not. And though this law may have been obscured by contrary practice, it has not yet been removed or impaired as far as nature and good manners are concerned; and so a man who behaves virtuously displays his nobility for all to see, and if anyone says otherwise it is they, and not the object of their discussion, who are at fault.

"Cast an eye over each of your noblemen, examine their way of life, their manners and their habits, and then look at those of Guiscardo: if you judge without prejudice you will pronounce him to be noble in the highest degree, and all these noblemen of yours to be mere louts. Concerning the virtues and merits of Guiscardo, I accepted no other counsel than yours, and that of my own eyes. No one praised him more than you did in all those commendable respects for which a worthy man deserves praise. And you were quite right to do so. For unless my eyes deceived me all the compliments you paid him were more than amply justified, as I saw it, by his own admirable conduct; and if I had been at all deceived in this it would have been by you alone. Will you still say that I have consorted with a man of ignoble character? If you do, you lie. But should you chance to call him a poor man, then I might concede the point, to your shame, since that is how you have seen fit to treat such a fine servant; but poverty deprives no one of nobility, only of wealth. Many a king, many a great prince was once poor, and many a ploughman or shepherd was once rich, and some still are.'"

his nobility more in his virtuous behaviour than in his ancestral pedigree:

... Coppo di Borghese Domenichi, il qual fu nella nostra città, e forse ancora è, uomo di grande e di reverenda autorità ne' dì nostri, e per costumi e per virtù, molto più che per nobiltà di sangue, chiarissimo e degno d'etterna fama, ...[142]

And Federigo degli Alberighi, the hero of the story that follows, also displays nobility, though impoverished, in his treatment of Monna Giovanna. Cisti the baker too, though of low estate, possesses the intelligence, wit and generosity of which real nobility is made:

Belle donne, io non so da me medesima vedere che più in questo si pecchi, o la natura apparecchiando ad una nobile anima un vil corpo, o la fortuna apparecchiando ad un corpo dotato d'anima nobile vil mestiero, sì come in Cisti nostro cittadino e in molti ancora abbiam potuto veder avvenire; il qual Cisti, d'altissimo animo fornito, la Fortuna fece fornaio.[143]

Finally there is the virtuous Griselda, whose dignity, gentility, patience and constancy belie her peasant background:

Ella era, come già dicemmo, di persona e di viso bella, e così come bella era, divenne tanto avvenevole, tanto piacevole e tanto costumata, che non figliuola di Giannucole e guardiana di pecore pareva stata, ma d'alcun nobile signore: di che

---

[142] *Decameron*, p. 669. '... Coppo di Borghese Domenichi, who dwelt in our city, and is perhaps alive there still, is greatly respected, and held in high esteem by his contemporaries. This most distinguished man deserves everlasting fame, not so much for his noble birth but rather for the virtue of his conduct, ...'

[143] Day VI, story 2 (*Decameron*, p. 706). 'Fair ladies, I cannot myself decide which is more at fault: nature, for lodging a noble soul in a miserable body, or fortune, for assigning a lowly trade to a body furnished with a noble spirit, which we have seen happen to our fellow citizen Cisti, and to many more besides. This Cisti was endowed with a soaring spirit, but fortune made him a baker.'

ella faceva maravigliare ogn'uom che prima conosciuta l'avea.[144]

Che si potrà dir qui, se non che anche nelle povere case piovono dal cielo de' divini spiriti, come nelle reali di quegli che sarien più degni di guardar porci che d'avere sopra uomini signoria?[145]

Thus we encounter once more in Boccaccio a progressive attitude whose implications could be said to reach down to the present century: the values of the meritocracy are already here in germ. But again we must take care not to distort the picture by projecting the characteristics of later developments back into Boccaccio himself. He is not egalitarian in the modern sense. For all their shortcomings and unfairness, he is prepared to accept the distinctions imposed on medieval society by birth, wealth and privilege as an inescapable part of the established order, the maintenance of which is essential to the harmony and well-being of society as a whole. He has no desire to challenge the recognised authorities, upset the *status quo* or disrupt the existing social hierarchy. It is simply that he does not recognise these divisions as divisions of merit: Boccaccio admires men and women for what they are in themselves, regardless of their status or position in society.

[144] Day X, story 10 (*Decameron*, pp. 1222–3). 'She was, as we have said, fair in face and limb, and she became as engaging, as charming and as well-mannered as she was beautiful, so that she seemed to be the daughter of some noble lord rather than of Giannucole the shepherd; and at this all those who had known her before were filled with wonderment.'

[145] The same story (*Decameron*, p. 1233). 'What is there left to say, except that heaven lets fall celestial spirits even into poor households, as it does into royal palaces some who are better suited to herding swine than to ruling over men?'

XVI

THE CHALLENGE OF FORTUNE

It was stated that one of the reasons for Boccaccio's admiration of human intelligence is that in addition to its function as a moral corrective it also constitutes man's only protection against the unpredictable vagaries of fortune. This is another of the purposes for which it was intended; it is a natural attribute divinely bestowed upon man to help him combat adversity:

> Manifesta cosa è che, sì come le cose temporali tutte sono transitorie e mortali, così in sé e fuor di sé essere piene di noia e d'angoscia e di fatica, e ad infiniti pericoli soggiacere; alle quali senza niuno fallo né potremmo noi, che viviamo mescolati in esse e che siamo parte d'esse, durare né ripararci, se spezial grazia di Dio forza e avvedimento non ci prestasse.[146]

Boccaccio reveals a constant preoccupation with fortune and its power over human life, not only in the *Decameron*[147]

---

[146] *Decameron*, Day I, story 1, pp. 46–7. 'It is clear that the things of this world are all transient and mortal, and that they are, moreover, beset both without and within by hardship, anguish and distress, and fraught with countless dangers; and we, whose lives are inseparably bound up in them, could neither endure them nor protect ourselves fully against them if strength and discernment were not granted to us by God's special grace.'

[147] The power of fortune over men's lives is emphasised from the outset in the description of the plague, and further accentuated in the proposal of the subject-matter for the stories of Day II: '. . . con ciò sia cosa che dal principio del mondo gli uomini sieno stati da diversi casi della fortuna menati, e saranno infino alla fine, ciascun debba dire sopra questo: Chi, da diverse cose infestato, sia, oltre alla sua speranza, riuscito a lieto fine.' (*Decameron*, Conclusion to Day I, p. 118.) '". . . as men have been subject to various twists of fate since the world began, and will be until it ends, all your stories should be on this subject: those who have been beset by various misfortunes, but whose adventures ended more happily than they dared to hope."' The stories of Days II, III, IV, V and

but also in the rest of his works. This is because it is a vital factor to be taken into account in man's quest for happiness in this life. Good fortune can bring man all the happiness he seeks. Ill fortune can ensure that he never finds it, however deserving, noble and virtuous he may be: that fortune is no respector of individual merit is clear from the circumstances of Guiscardo[148] and of Cisti.[149] Though Boccaccio does not discount the possibility of divine intervention in human affairs (as is apparent from his suggestion that the plague may have been a divine visitation upon the wicked citizens of Florence),[150] fortune in the *Decameron* is not for the most part the operation of divine providence: it is the blind and arbitrary workings of pure chance, a random pattern of events, aimless and without purpose, determined only by the casual interplay of the natural forces of the contingent universe.

It is against the twists and turns of such forces as these that man is compelled to pit his wits, courage and enterprise if he is to avert possible disaster and attain his desired goal. Fate can never be fully subdued to human will, and man remains ultimately something of a puppet at the mercy of its ups and downs, its fickle whims, its bewildering fluctuations and reversals (as the preposterous changes of fortune in the stories of adventure show).[151] It is not, therefore, a question of man dominating fortune through the use of his own intelligence, as it was to be for later humanists like Alberti,[152] but rather of learning by

---

VI are nearly all concerned with this theme, as the relevant headings to the individual days' narrations show.

[148] See chapter xv, pp. 86–8.   [149] See p 89.   [150] See note 15 above.

[151] For examples of the vicissitudes of fortune, and their effect on human life in such stories, see note 156 below.

[152] 'Tiene gioco la fortuna solo a chi se gli sottomette.' (L. B. Alberti, *I Libri della Famiglia*, in *Opere Volgari*, edited by C. Grayson, Laterza, Bari, 1960; the statement occurs in the Prologue, p. 6).

experience how to adapt oneself to circumstances as they occur. Man's chances are only fifty-fifty. No amount of planning and foresight can fully safeguard against mishap, and even the cleverest and most prudent man can come to grief if the fates are completely hostile. Fortune overcomes all human resistance, and frustrates all our best laid plans at times. The plague is a case in point: no amount of intelligent forethought was able to avert the epidemic.

E in quella non valendo alcuno senno né umano provvedimento, per lo quale fu da molte immondizie purgata la città da oficiali sopra ciò ordinati e vietato l'entrarvi dentro a ciascuno infermo e molti consigli dati a conservazion della sanità, né ancora umili supplicazioni non una volta ma molte e in processioni ordinate e in altre guise a Dio fatte dalle divote persone, quasi nel principio della primavera dell'anno predetto orribilmente cominciò i suoi dolorosi effetti, e in miracolosa maniera, a dimostrare.[153]

There are further examples from the stories of men suffering ill fortune, irrespective of whether they have been wise or foolish: in the eighth tale of Day II the Count of Antwerp is falsely accused; in the third *novella* of Day V Pietro Boccamazza is captured by brigands; and in the first story of Day X Ruggieri de' Figiovanni is cheated of great wealth when he has the bad luck to choose the wrong chest. But, for all this, we do still have more than a sporting chance if we play our cards right. We should not seek to resist fortune: that is to court disaster. Rather we should go along with it and learn from experience

[153] Introduction to Day I (*Decameron*, p. 13). 'But no human wit or forethought was of any avail against it; for although the city was cleansed of much filth by officials appointed for the purpose, and any sick person was forbidden entry, and many instructions were issued to safeguard public health; and despite the humble supplication made to God by devout believers, not once but many times, in orderly processions and in other ways, the spring of the aforenamed year had scarcely begun when it started to manifest its awesome, grievous and terrifying symptoms.'

how to become resilient, how to ride out the storms and remain alert to opportunities when they present themselves, so that we may profit by any good fortune that happens to come our way in between times.

There are many instances in the stories of people who manage to survive ill fortune and come out of it all right in the end, either by luck or by their own efforts. The stories of Day II are specifically concerned with this theme,[154] and the fourth and fifth tales of this series (the tales of Landolfo Rufolo and Andreuccio da Perugia) are among the better examples. A similar case is that of Messer Torello in the ninth tale of Day X. The most convincing illustrations, however, are those where clever people, oppressed by fate, manage to turn ill fortune to their advantage. Specific instances of people seizing opportunities of averting disaster, or turning bad fortune to good through their own intelligence and initiative, occur in the third story of Day I (Melchisedech averts the menace of Saladin),[155] in the fourth *novella* of the same day

[154] See the heading to the stories of Day II: 'Finisce la prima giornata del Decameron: incomincia la seconda, nella quale, sotto il reggimento di Filomena, si ragiona di chi, da diverse cose infestato, sia oltre alla sua speranza riuscito a lieto fine.' (Introduction to Day II, *Decameron*, p. 123.) 'Here ends the first day of the *Decameron*, and the second begins, in which, under the rule of Filomena, the discussion concerns those who have been beset by various misfortunes, but whose adventures ended more happily than they dared to hope.' The same applies to the tales of the fifth day, which is introduced thus: 'Finisce la quarta giornata del Decameron; incomincia la quinta, nella quale, sotto il reggimento di Fiammetta, si ragiona di ciò che ad alcuno amante, dopo alcuni fieri o sventurati accidenti, felicemente avvenisse.' (Introduction to Day V, *Decameron*, p. 575.) 'Here ends the fourth day of the *Decameron*, and the fifth begins, in which, under the rule of Fiammetta, the discussion concerns the adventures of lovers whose cruel misfortunes had a happy ending.'

[155] 'Voi dovete, amorose compagne, sapere che, sì come la sciocchezza spesse volte trae altrui di felice stato e mette in grandissima miseria, così il senno di grandissimi pericoli trae il savio e ponlo in grande e in sicuro riposo. E che vero sia che la sciocchezza di buono stato in miseria altrui conduca, per molti essempli si vede, li quali non fia al presente nostra cura di raccontare, avendo riguardo che tutto 'l dì mille essempli n'appaiano manifesti: ma che il senno di consolazione sia cagione, come promisi,

(where the monk escapes censure for his lust by taking advantage of his knowledge of the abbot's similar misdemeanours), in the first of Day III (the resourcefulness of the frustrated nuns) and—perhaps the best example of all —in the tenth tale of Day VI (Fra Cipolla and the coals).[156] The importance which Boccaccio attaches to this theme is indicated by the fact that it is designated as the subject of the stories both of Day III[157] and of Day VI.[158]

---

per una novelletta mosterrò brievemente.' (*Decameron*, pp. 74-5.) 'You should know, my loving companions, that just as stupidity often drags the fool from his good fortune, and casts him into utter wretchedness, so perspicacity extricates the wise man from grave perils, and leaves him in calm and secure repose. We see many instances of the way stupidity leads men into misfortune, and I do not intend to tell you of them now, seeing that they are such common occurrences. I shall tell you instead, as I promised, a little story that shows in few words what a comfort perspicacity is to a man.'

[156] Many of the tales concerned with fortune are tales of adventure with longish, rambling plots (comparatively speaking) that are reminiscent of the chivalrous romance tradition, to which many of them originally belong. Good examples occur especially in the stories of Day II and in a fair number of those of Day III (for example, stories 7 and 9), of Day IV (for example, stories 2, 3, 4 and 10), of Day V (particularly stories 1, 2, 3, 7 and 8) and of Day X (story 9, for instance).

[157] See the Conclusion to Day II (*Decameron*, p. 308): '"Quivi quando noi saremo domenica appresso dormire adunati, avendo noi oggi avuto assai largo spazio da discorrere ragionando, sì perché più tempo da pensare avrete e sì perché sarà ancora più bello che un poco si ristringa del novellare la licenzia e che sopra uno de' molti fatti della fortuna si dica, i' ho pensato che questo sarà: di chi alcuna cosa molto da lui desiderata con industria acquistasse, o la perduta recuperasse."' '"As we have had a very free rein for our discussions today, and as you will have had more time to think when we forgather on Sunday, after our siesta, at our new abode, I believe it would be better for us to restrict the freedom of our tales a little, and to tell of one of the many aspects of fortune; and I have decided that it shall be: those who by their own endeavours gained something which they greatly prized, or won back what they had lost."'

[158] See the Conclusion to Day V (*Decameron*, p. 692): '"Noi abbiamo già molte volte udito che con be' motti e con risposte pronte o con avvedimenti presti molti hanno già saputo con debito morso rintuzzare gli altrui denti o i sopravegnenti pericoli cacciar via; e per ciò che la materia è bella e può essere utile, voglio che domane, con l'aiuto di Dio, infra questi termini si ragioni, cioè di chi, con alcuno leggiadro motto tentato, si riscosse, o con pronta risposta o avvedimento fuggì perdita, pericolo o

There is a parallel between the course of action thus advocated and the concept of natural morality. Here too we have a balance of nature and reason: to follow fortune intelligently is like following nature reasonably. In each case it is a matter of accepting the existing conditions of the natural order of which we are ourselves a part, and of learning to adapt ourselves to them. In either context the learning of this lesson is the sign of real intelligence and the mark of true wisdom.

It may thus be observed that the view of fortune which Boccaccio here advances rules out the possibility of a strict determinism (the individual retains his own free will and his capacity for independent action despite the conditioning effect of his environment)[159] and by the same token discounts rigid notions of predestination, whether religious or astrological in origin. However, as we have seen, divine providence is never finally excluded from the scheme of things (for an orthodox Christian this would have been an untenable position), and it is interesting to perceive how Boccaccio reconciles his own conception of fortune as a wayward and capricious agency, haphazard and erratic in its activities, with the Christian belief in a providential God. A compromise is envisaged, in which the workings of chance and the action of providence are seen to coexist and complement each other. Boccaccio acknowledges a general kind of predestination in the belief, expressed both in the *Decameron* and in the *Gene-*

---

scorno."' '"We have already often heard that many people have managed to put others firmly in their place, or to avert impending dangers, by witty remarks and swift ripostes, or by means of their alertness; and as it is a fine subject, and may be useful to you, I want you, with God's help, to concentrate on it tomorrow, and to tell of those who, when put to the test by a clever quip, were able to return the compliment, or who escaped loss, danger or disgrace by a ready retort or swift perception."'

[159] See chapter VIII, pp. 36–7.

alogie Deorum Gentilium Libri, that the universe was designed by God for a purpose, and that that purpose still
directs it.[160] To a medieval Christian like Boccaccio this
purpose could only be the creation and redemption of
mankind. But, notwithstanding his belief in a divinely
ordained plan for the salvation of man, Boccaccio suggests that God refrains, on the whole, from direct intervention in human affairs, and in the workings of the
material universe generally, and simply allows his creation
to work according to the laws by which it was originally
created: the laws of nature. In other words, having set up
the system he is content, for the most part, to let it run
itself. This is the implication of the passage from the
Genealogie Deorum Gentilium Libri previously examined:

Et si ab ipsa natura, que sic celos, sic astrorum orbes et cursus
varia etiam agitatione disposuit, agente Deo, ut *nullo labore suo*
[my italics] ad officia productos varia nos videmus, . . .[161]

Direct intervention by God would therefore seem to be
envisaged only in exceptional circumstances (the birth of
Christ, and, possibly, the plague). Furthermore chance
and coincidence, resulting from the interaction of the
forces of the natural order, are an inescapable part of the
universe he has created. So Boccaccio's interpretation of
providence is one which admits of the existence of chance
in particular circumstances within the system, while re-
taining the belief in an overall guiding intelligence.

[160] See the passage from Day X, story 8, quoted on p. 40: the story
concerns ancient Rome, so the reference is to the pagan gods of antiquity,
but the principle is the same.
[161] *Genealogie Deorum Gentilium Libri*, book xv, chapter 10. See the
translation of the passage on p. 16 (note 29).

XVII

SUMMING UP

In the foregoing chapters the central moral issue has been indicated, and a number of particular aspects have been identified, and considered, as individual reflections of a general principle. It may perhaps enable us to see Boccaccio's values in clearer historical perspective if we endeavour now to draw up some sort of balance sheet. Hitherto in this analysis the question of the medieval or Renaissance character of these values has been, for the most part, a secondary consideration. The attempt at a systematic definition of Boccaccio's attitudes in terms of Middle Ages and Renaissance has been avoided as far as possible, in order to preclude the dangers of preconception. Now that an initial survey has been made, however, some such clarification should be feasible. Any exercise of this sort must remain at best a tentative one. Approximate equations are all that is possible in the circumstances, for there is, of course, no absolute watershed between the Middle Ages and the Renaissance: only a very gradual, prolonged and almost imperceptible transition from one to the other. But if categoric solutions are rejected, the undertaking is not without its uses.

In general terms, Boccaccio's secular outlook, his adherence to nature, his enlightened and liberal attitudes, his broadmindedness, sympathy and tolerance all present an appreciable contrast to the ascetic tenor of much medieval ethics, the artificiality of many existing moral conventions, the strictness and severity that frequently characterised their enforcement, and the narrowness and rigidity of outlook that often lay behind them. In this he clearly foreshadows the Renaissance (though he is not, of course, by any means alone in doing so). Similarly his recognition of the need for some reasonable restraint of natural instinct, to be achieved through the enlightened exercise of the intellect, can be said to anticipate the rationalism of later Renaissance writers like Ariosto and Montaigne, and to require a degree of self-consciousness and self-awareness that is another frequent feature of Renaissance activities. The conception of virtue that emerges from this discipline (positing as it does the individual's ability to determine his conduct through the exercise of his own free will, and arising out of the self-sufficiency and sense of personal responsibility of the fulfilled and contented man) similarly reflects the self-confidence of the Renaissance and its faith in the capacities of the individual.

In more specific terms, his permissive attitude to love represents a conscious departure from the repressive approach of the medieval Church. His comparatively enlightened attitude to marriage in the *Decameron*, and to the place of women in society as a whole, is a foretaste of the *Cortegiano* and the cultured ladies of the Renaissance who figure therein (though his advocacy of courtesy and consideration in the treatment of women is at the same time clearly influenced by the medieval code of chivalry and courtly love). His criticisms of the corruptions of the clergy are part of a long medieval tradition, but here too he displays an understanding of their predicament, and a recognition of the difficulty of keeping to their ascetic ideal, that sound a new note. His admiration of intelligence, education and culture derives largely from the humanist's faith in the powers of the individual human intellect and belief in the ennobling powers of scholarship (though once again there is an essential continuity here with medieval culture: compare, for example, the *dolce stil novo*'s equation of nobility with scholarship and the intellect).[162] His suggestion that human intelligence can be used constructively to minimise the perils of fortune, and to exploit promising opportunities to the full, is symptomatic of the spirit of enterprise and self-reliance that also characterises so much Renaissance thought and action. The celebration of courtesy is, at one and the same time, a development of the medieval code of chivalry and courtly love and an anticipation of the ideal of courtesy that finds expression in the *Cortegiano* and the *Galateo*. His conception of nobility, like his conception of intelligence, reflects the humanist idea of the nobility of the intellect and the ennobling effects of culture. It also reflects the democratic and republican sympathies of the Florentine bourgeoisie (though Boccaccio rejects the bourgeois association of nobility with wealth in favour of the humanist idea of the nobility of the intellect). There are again, however, recognisable medieval elements here: the chivalrous virtues of gallantry, gentility, courtesy and magnanimity are essential ingredients of nobility. And even the fundamental idea that nobility is a matter of character, rather than of rank or wealth, has a well established medieval precedent in Guittone d'Arezzo and in the *dolce stil novo*. This is because the values of Guittone, the *stilnovisti* and Boccaccio were all influenced by the republicanism of the

---

[162] It is interesting to note in this connection that the activities of story-telling and discussion, which fulfil such a central function in the cultural and moral education of the narrators, are themselves the reflection of a social fashion that has its roots in the culture of the early Middle Ages but which, like courtly love and like the code of chivalry (for which see pp. 102–3, and note 164 below), not only survived the transition from Middle Ages to Renaissance but developed and expanded to become an established part of the new culture. For a closer consideration of the history and significance of story-telling and discussion in social gatherings see the appendix.

medieval communes of north and central Italy, a social
and political system that had its origins far back in the
tenth century but which was, right from its inception, an
integral part of the developing Renaissance, for it was in
these medieval communes that the Italian Renaissance
was born.

Boccaccio's attitude to fortune, too, belongs in
different ways both to the Middle Ages and to the Renaissance. Divine providence is still envisaged as a factor in
the shaping of human affairs, and Boccaccio does not yet
entirely rule out the influence of the stars either: the
plague, he suggests, could have been due to the disposition of the heavens, or it may have been God's visitation
upon the wicked.[163] The religious and astrological ex-
planations advanced in the Introduction to Day I still
retain a marked medieval flavour, though the astrological
hypothesis does at least imply natural causes of a sort.
But, broadly speaking, Boccaccio's interpretation of fortune in the *Decameron* is closer to that of later Renaissance
writers than to medieval theories of predestination and
free will. It is not based primarily on transcendental, providential or astrological considerations. Generally, human
life is neither determined by the movements of the
heavens nor governed directly by the will of God. Fortune to Boccaccio is, for the most part, the classical and
Renaissance *fortuna*: fate, the product of natural causes, of
the forces of man's immediate environment, the physical
world around him; and as such it is essentially arbitrary
and undirected. And man's defence against fortune lies
principally in himself, in his own intelligence, courage and

---

[163] See chapter II, p. 8, and note 15 above. A similar conjunction of the
action of divine providence and of the influence of the stars in determining
the patterns of human existence may possibly be implied in the passage
from the *Genealogie Deorum Gentilium Libri* quoted on p. 97.

resilience. Thus Boccaccio's interpretation throws the onus of responsibility for determining one's fate on the personal initiative of the individual, and on his capacity for self-reliance. Man can already be seen in the *Decameron* to be striving to shape his own destiny, as far as prevailing circumstances will permit. He cannot *ensure* that things will work out well for him, no matter how hard he tries; but it is nevertheless up to him, and to no one else, to extricate himself from such misfortunes as he encounters, using his own God-given intelligence and native wit. Boccaccio here foreshadows both Alberti and Machiavelli; but it is with Machiavelli that he has most in common, for he too gives man only a fifty-fifty chance of success in his battle against fortune, whereas Alberti expresses the belief that man can actually dominate fate and rule his own destiny if he is strong enough.

The most obvious medieval feature in Boccaccio's values is the code of chivalry, as embodied in characters like Federigo degli Alberighi. This derives ultimately from the code of conduct of the feudal knight. But in Boccaccio it is no longer chivalry as it was originally conceived by the feudal barons of the early Middle Ages (a code of martial prowess and aristocratic honour). It is imbued with the culture, civilization and refinement, the courtesy and gallantry associated with the code of courtly love, as evolved in the courts of Provence, inherited by medieval and Renaissance Italy, and interpreted in the medieval literary traditions of lyric poetry and chivalrous romance. It is the code of chivalry in the refined, idealised form in which it was to survive all the way through the Renaissance: chivalry and courtesy as envisaged later at the Renaissance court of Ferrara, where it is reflected in the works of the court poets Boiardo, Ariosto and Tasso;

and as interpreted in the courtesy books of Castiglione and Della Casa.[164]

The picture that emerges from this somewhat cursory review tends to confirm the image of Boccaccio as a transitional figure. Medieval values still play a great part in the shaping of Boccaccio's standards in the *Decameron*. But there is nevertheless already discernible the nucleus of a new kind of morality, fundamentally different from the traditional standards of the past. The conventional moral values propagated by the medieval Church, and by the society of feudalism, both in their different ways exert an important formative influence on the development of the very attitudes that outgrow them: from medieval Christianity Boccaccio inherits his compassionate and

[164] As the feudalism of the Middle Ages waned there grew up, among the cultured members of the courts of Italy, a feeling of nostalgia for the ideals of medieval chivalry. At first this cult of chivalry would have been found principally among the aristocracy, who looked back longingly to the 'good old days' when their authority was undisputed and their standards were the accepted norm throughout the higher echelons of society (the court of King Robert of Naples provides an example of such a setting in Boccaccio's own time). But it also spread to the ruling bourgeois merchant families and their entourage, who had largely replaced the old feudal aristocracy in the republics and *signorie* of north and central Italy and who, like all social climbers, sought to secure their new-found position of power and prestige in society by assimilating the values and adopting the customs and civilisation of their erstwhile superiors, with whom they had now become increasingly identified. Thus the new ruling classes found a touchstone for the refined manners and culture to which they aspired in the chivalry and courtesy of the courtly civilisation of the early Middle Ages (that is, in the established standards of the society that had preceded them). The nostalgia for the values of a vanishing age that was such an important factor in this cult of chivalry meant that the image of that code of conduct which survived was a romantic and idealised one. The world of chivalry itself (the feudal society of the early Middle Ages) was long dead, at least in the city States of north and central Italy. What lived on into the later Middle Ages and the Renaissance was a romantic vision of an ideal world of love, courtesy, nobility and honour, education and culture: a fantasy world, a world of the imagination, in which all the ladies were fair and charming and all the knights gallant and bold. It was, in short, the world of chivalrous romance. Notice how many of Boccaccio's preoccupations are part of this world and of the chivalrous ideal upon which it resided: love, courtesy, nobility, education and culture.

charitable instincts,[165] and the legacy of feudalism is apparent in his admiration of chivalry and courtesy, and in his love of courtly refinement.[166] But in the *Decameron* this medieval inheritance is absorbed, assimilated and finally transcended: the emphasis changes, the centre of attention is transferred, and the new total is somehow greater than the sum of its constituent parts. Thus it is that the *Decameron*, written in the medieval literary convention of the *novella*, has paradoxically more of the attitudes and values of the Renaissance than Boccaccio's later works of humanist scholarship.

Such values did not, however, develop in a vacuum. Boccaccio is only reflecting the attitudes prevalent in the social milieux in which he moved, for, like everyone else, he too is a product of his background. There would appear to be two decisive influences here. The first is that of the courtly society of Naples, under Robert of Anjou, where Boccaccio spent a great deal of his youth and early manhood: the civilised, sophisticated, cultured, worldly and pleasure-loving society that bequeathed the idealised code of chivalry and courtesy to Renaissance Italy. The second is that of the educated Florentine bourgeoisie, the *popolo grasso* or rich merchant classes, into which he was born and to which he returned from Naples in 1341.[167] From his stay in Naples Boccaccio probably retained the pleasure-loving attitudes of the young courtiers and nobles (the men and women of the *gaie brigate* that Boccaccio is supposed to have frequented, and which are remembered in the *Filocolo*—Fiammetta's garden—and in the settings of the *Ninfale d'Ameto* and the *Decameron* itself); he retains also the medieval love of chivalry

---

[165] See chapter XII, p. 68.   [166] See pp. 102–3 and note 164 above.
[167] The young men and women of the *cornice* all appear to be typical representatives of this aspiring and cultured Florentine bourgeoisie.

as it was cultivated in Naples (the courtly and chivalrous traditions having remained stronger there than in north and central Italy, partly because of the strong feudal culture imported into Naples from northern France under Angevin rule); and his love of education and culture, his admiration of intelligence and his idea of the nobility of letters owe much to the influence of early humanist scholars, with whom Boccaccio would have come into contact in Naples, and who must have played a significant part in his own education.[168] Finally, the prominent function assigned to story-telling and discussion in the educative process suggested by the cultural activities of the narrators in the *cornice* of the *Decameron* is almost certainly due initially to the author's direct participation in such activities at the Neopolitan court, from which experience the germ of the *Decameron* probably emerged.[169]

From the society of the educated Florentine middle classes, on the other hand, Boccaccio doubtless inherits much of his liberal, enlightened and tolerant attitude, and his secular and worldy outlook (in particular his sound common sense, which recalls the practical spirit and hard-headed commercial realism of the merchant). In addition, the qualities of decency (*onestà*) and moderation (*misura*) contained in his conception of virtue are recognisable bourgeois virtues that became increasingly valued as the Middle Ages developed into the Renaissance, and the rich merchant classes increased their dominance of civic society. This background also helps to explain his

[168] Naples was an important centre of early humanism: Paolo da Perugia, Bernard Barlaam and Dionigi da Borgo San Sepolcro were all associated with the Angevin court there in Robert's time. Thus it is that Boccaccio's culture already shows signs of humanist propensities before the historic meeting with Petrarch in 1351, which served to reinforce existing interests rather than to effect a conversion .

[169] See the appendix.

emphasis on individual intelligence and personal initiative, especially in dealing with fortune. The medieval merchants were among the first to develop, in response to the challenges and hazards of commerce, the spirit of enterprise and self-reliance, the self-confidence and faith in one's own judgement and ability, that are conventionally associated with Renaissance society as a whole. The Boccaccian protagonist pitting his wits against fate is strongly reminiscent of the medieval trader, risking goods and capital to sell his wares and make his profit, confronted by a formidable array of obstacles (the elements, pirates, brigands, taxes and levies, fluctuations in the market, bankruptcies and so forth), and with nothing but his own judgement and determination to see him through. Notice how many of the stories of fortune and intelligence concern merchants,[170] and how many involve travel and adventure, often abroad and overseas, with all the hazards this entails.[171] Similarly one may cite Boccaccio's conception of nobility and his republican sympathies as further attitudes inherited from his middle-class Florentine background; even the love of medieval chivalry and courtesy instilled in Naples seems likely to have been reinforced by the cultural enthusiasm of the educated and aspiring bourgeoisie for the old chivalrous ideal.[172] Lastly, we should remember that his idea of the educative value of story-telling and discussion probably received a similar reinforcement from the popularity of such pursuits among the more leisured and cultivated members of the Florentine middle classes.[173]

This consideration of the Florentine bourgeois origins

[170] For example, Day I, story 3; Day II, stories 3 and 5; Day VIII, story 10, and Day X, story 9.

[171] For example, Day II, stories 4, 6 ,7, 8 and 9; Day IV, stories 3 and 4; Day V, stories 1, 2 and 3, and Day X, story 9.

[172] See note 164 above.   [173] See the appendix.

of Boccaccio's values reveals one thing above all others: that the progressive outlook of the author of the *Decameron* is not that of a visionary or prophet, of a man born ahead of his time. Boccaccio remains very much a man of the fourteenth century, a typical product of his age, for even his most radical ideas are ultimately nothing more than the natural reflection of attitudes prevalent among the more advanced, enterprising and forward-looking sections of the late medieval Italian society to which he himself belonged.[174] If Boccaccio appears to us in the *Decameron* as a transitional figure it is because he lived in a transitional age.

In the final analysis, however, it is not the discussion of the medieval or Renaissance nature of Boccaccio's views, or the question of their social provenance, that most commands our attention. It is simply the message of the author himself to his readers: the declaration that to be at ease with life and with oneself, to find fulfilment in the responsible exercise of one's natural functions, is the means to achieve the happy and virtuous life to which all men are entitled. It is an eminently sound and sensible conclusion, a supremely normal, wholesome and realistic

[174] The merchant classes of the city States of north and central Italy appear to us now to have been the very life-blood of the Renaissance. Throughout the transition the activities and attitudes of these merchants played a key part in the new developments. Their profits literally created and subsidised the Renaissance, providing the wealth that made possible the patronage of scholarship, literature and the arts. They were largely responsible too for shaping the *spirit* of the Renaissance. Through travel and international trade they helped to spread culture and ideas, and hence to broaden people's horizons generally (whence the new objectivity, relativism, understanding and tolerance). Their practical wordly interests and their active involvement in society encouraged a greater interest in the things of this life (whence the new secular spirit); and the harsh realities of travel and commerce required courage, foresight and a firm belief in oneself (whence the new spirit of initiative and self-reliance). All these qualities are inherent, as we have seen, in the attitudes of the author of the *Decameron*.

attitude, a message that is infinitely refreshing, reassuring, sane and wise. And the *Decameron* reflects it at every turn. It is bursting with gaiety and mirth, vitality and vigour, gusto and enthusiasm. It radiates *joie de vivre*, cheerful, good-humoured optimism, exuberant high spirits, a rollicking, rumbustious sense of fun, a great appetite for experience and flair for living, and an immense capacity for enjoying life and all that it has to offer. There is in the *Decameron* a joyous acceptance of life in all its manifestations, but also, underlying it, a dignity and maturity of outlook born of a profound understanding of human nature and a proper appreciation of human needs.

APPENDIX

DISCUSSION GROUPS

The fashion for meeting in groups to indulge in debate on a variety of topics, or simply to tell stories (and often, as in the *Decameron*, to do both), was a popular practice of the day that seems to have originated in the courts of the feudal aristocracy of Provence and northern France at about the start of the twelfth century, and to have been imported into Italy, like the code of chivalry and courtly love, via the south: first into Sicily under the Swabians, where the dominant cultural influence was that of Provence, and then into Naples under the Angevins, who brought with them from northern France their feudal cultural traditions. By the later Middle Ages and Renaissance it had spread to the courts of the *signorie* and the households of the well-to-do merchants and upper middle classes in the municipalities of north and central Italy (an instance of the cultural assimilation described in note 164 above).

These discussion groups had thus become an integral part of the culture of the time, and exerted a considerable influence on literature. They were instrumental in the elevation of the *novella* from the popular to the literary plane, as it was largely because of them that story-telling became a popular diversion of the educated and literate; and this development of the *novella* as a literary genre from story-telling in discussion groups is reflected in the frequent retention of the motif of the discussion group itself (or of some similar gathering) as a general setting for the stories. Of this feature the *cornice* of the *Decameron* is a prime example. Boccaccio is in fact particularly attached to this setting, for he had already made use of it in the *Filocolo* and in the *Ninfale d'Ameto*. It is probable that he participated in such gatherings in Naples and Florence (see pp. 104–6), and this experience doubtless played a significant part in the genesis of the *Decameron*. Not only does it appear to have given him the idea for the setting of the work, but it is also likely that it provided him with a good deal of the material of the actual stories. In addition to the *novella* the discussion groups were also partly responsible for the development of a series of written dialogues, which presumably grew out of the more serious discussions in such groups (though here classical precedent also plays an important part): courtesy books like the *Cortegiano* of Castiglione and the *Galateo* of Della Casa (the latter is actually a monologue), and philosophical dialogues like the *Famiglia* of Alberti.

The earlier medieval discussion groups had been concerned mainly with numerous doubts and queries regarding love. These 'questions of love' were the product of the courtly culture of Provence, and were subsequently taken up also in Palermo and Naples. They were subtle intellectual discussions between courtiers and ladies on various aspects of love as interpreted in the prevailing code of courtly love. Although influenced to some extent by the techniques of scholastic dialectic, they were not primarily of an academic nature but were intended principally to provide the court with an interesting cultural pastime. As such, they were part of the culture of feudalism, and closely associated with medieval lyric poetry (in particular with the disputative form of the *tenzone*), since both were developments of courtly love as evolved in Provence. Examples of questions of love are to be found in the episode of Fiammetta's garden in the *Filocolo*. Subsequently story-telling came to play an increasingly important part in the activities of the groups. The original aim of the stories was probably, as in the *Filocolo*, the illustration of questions under discussion, and so they would be of an instructive nature, though seldom very serious. Then the habit of swapping stories presumably developed for its own sake, for entertainment and for general interest, although the didactic element was retained to some extent, because of the firm medieval conviction, reinforced by the *exemplum* tradition of the Church, that every story should point a moral of some sort. This development is reflected in the *Decameron*, where the *novelle* still have an illustrative function, with the narrators often stating the moral of a tale, but where this aspect is more a subordinate one than in the *Filocolo*, as the main aim of the stories is now entertainment.

This trend towards light-hearted entertainment is tempered somewhat by the kinds of discussion we see reflected in a number of dialogues of the high Renaissance, where story-telling is not to the fore, and discussion of more serious philosophical, political, social and cultural issues is the central focus of attention. Often these are of a dry, scholarly nature, and owe more to the study of antiquity than to current social fashions. But often, too, an air of festivity survives, reminiscent of the atmosphere of the gatherings that still inspire and condition the works in some cases (in the *Cortegiano* for example); and the less weighty tradition of engaging conversation, story-telling and light-hearted discussion continues in the high Renaissance on both the social and the literary plane (as we can see from the *novelle* of Bandello), riddles and parlour games being added to the list of other more obviously cultural activities that seem habitually to have accompanied the debates (see note 129 above).

Although love, and especially Platonic love, was still a dominant theme in these later debates, the scope of the discussion was far wider than in the earlier ones, where courtly love had been an almost exclusive preoccupation. It is possible that this broadening of scope was partly the result of the development of story-telling as an end in itself, because of the wide range of subject-matter in the tales. However, it is at the same time unquestionably a sign of the tremendous expansion of horizons in the Renaissance in contrast to the narrow, enclosed world of the Provençal courts.

For further information on discussion groups see T. F. Crane, *Italian Social Customs of the Sixteenth Century and their Influence on the Literatures of Europe*, Yale University Press, New Haven, and Oxford University Press, London, 1920.

INDEX

The index is divided into two parts: the first contains a list of historical figures, authors, characters, places and works of literature mentioned in the book; the second contains references to individual sections of the *Decameron*.